THE NATURE OF
TRUSTEESHIP

The Role and Responsibilities of College and University Boards

John W. Nason

THE NATURE OF
TRUSTEESHIP

*The Role and Responsibilities of
College and University Boards*

John W. Nason

Robert L. Gale
President, Association of
Governing Boards of
Universities and Colleges

Foreword

College trusteeship, like every other aspect of higher education, has felt the enormous pressures generated by a variety of social forces ever since World War II, when the GI Bill suddenly opened college doors to large new clienteles. Yet, until the campus turmoil of the 1960s, not a great deal of attention, scholarly or other, was devoted to trusteeship. Many student demonstrators searching for the center of power were baffled to discover that the pinnacle of authority on campus seemed to be a reputedly somnolent panel of elderly men who met rather rarely and made little news when they did.

Yet the students turned a spotlight on the institution of college trusteeship, and in the decade of the '70s a sudden onset of financial problems intensified the glare on boards that had long enjoyed an honorable obscurity. Students of higher education, along with the media and the public, began to take an interest. Much of their comment was critical, and some students and faculty went so far as to propose substitution of faculty/student control of the campus. Few of those knowledgeable about our higher education institutions and their problems of governance took such suggestions seriously, and this uniquely American system by which some 38,000 volunteer citizens accept ultimate responsibility for our 3,250 public and private campuses remains unshaken.

Among the scholars who began examining trusteeship in the 1970s was one very special group, recruited by the Association of Governing Boards to serve on its Commission on the Future. Seven distinguished leaders in higher education contributed their views in a series of essays covering the problems of trusteeship in the various categories of institutions. Dr. John W. Nason, executive director of the Commission, then undertook the project's major work. In addition to the seven essays he was able to make use of two other important resources: a nationwide survey of trustees and presidents conducted in 1973-74 by J.A. Davis, Director of the Center for Educational Research and Evaluation of the Research Triangle Institute, assisted by Steve A. Batchelor; and a series of regional conferences in which presidents, board chairmen, and trustees exchanged views. Dr. Nason's report, entitled *The Future of Trusteeship*, was published by AGB in the spring of 1975 and has been continuously in demand since.

Now, seven years later, Dr. Nason has undertaken a complete revision of his book. There are two major reasons for the revision. First, a great deal of new scholarly material has become available from the research of the past seven years. Second, the role of the trustee has been substantially—and, in a great many cases, dramatically—altered and broadened. The urgency and sense of the financial crisis that has deepened even further in the '80s for both private and public higher education have forced governing boards into a far more active interest in all aspects of institutional costs; from deferral of maintenance to reduction of academic programs, as well as everything affecting institutional revenues, from tuition increases to the budget struggles in the state and national capitols. Not surprisingly, Dr. Nason has found it necessary to enlarge his list of trustees' basic responsibilities from 10 to 13.

The original edition of *The Future of Trusteeship* was immediately recognized as a classic in 1975. This new edition—more aptly titled *The Nature of Trusteeship*, to indicate that it is more than a mere revision—will, we hope, prove to be even more useful to trustees and presidents, indeed to everyone with an interest in the governance and well-being of our colleges and universities.

Acknowledgment

I am grateful to the Association of Governing Boards for involving me in the study of college and university trustees. The original invitation came from J.L. Zwingle, then president of AGB, and the Association's Commission on the Future. The original funding was generously provided by the Carnegie Corporation of New York.

Having been a trustee and a president, I began with some knowledge of the perennial problems of trusteeship and of its changing nature. The present volume is a distillation of what I have learned from nine years of concentrated study and writing.

During those years I have profited from the constant encouragement and support of the AGB staff and board of directors. I have worked closely and happily with Robert L. Gale, president; Richard T. Ingram, executive vice president; Nancy R. Axelrod, vice president for programs and public policy; Linda Henderson, coordinator of the Trustee Information Service; and Joseph C. Gies, editor. They and their associates are a remarkable team, and I owe them more than they will ever know.

John W. Nason
Keene, New York
June 1982

Table of Contents

1

THE ACIDS OF MODERNITY

In times of great stress, when values are up for grabs and when an increasing number of allocative decisions in society are made at more complex levels than simple consumer choice, the great symbolic institutions of our past stabilities are bound to be challenged from within and without. …Whiplashed by those who fear change and by those who crave it, our great institutions of governance and education find it difficult to define their goals or save their souls.

Stephen K. Bailey (1973)

This study is an examination of the role and responsibilities of college and university trustees in the last quarter of the twentieth century. It is not a treatise on the complex and sometimes Byzantine governance of colleges and universities, but an analysis of the problems and opportunities of governing boards.

The members of those governing boards constitute an extraordinary group of approximately 38,000 men and women who, without compensation, devote time, intelligence, emotional energy, and money to the welfare of the 3,250 post-secondary institutions for which they are responsible. Some are appointed by state or local officials, some by religious orders or denominations; some get elected by public vote and some are chosen by the alumni associations; some are co-opted by self-perpetuating boards. With relatively few exceptions they are lay persons.

In most countries higher education is controlled by one or more government agencies staffed by professional educators. Some universities, such as Oxford and Cambridge, give faculty and administration almost complete responsibility. But in the United States the governance of higher education has been shared among trustees, administrators, and faculty. In recent years students have also participated in a few institutions.

An Historical Perspective

Each of the three groups (excluding students) has tended to dominate the governance at different periods, and a brief historical sketch will illuminate the present situation.

In the eighteenth and nineteenth centuries trustees were dominant. Until the Civil War

3

growth in higher education had been very slow. By 1870 total college and university enrollment had reached 50,000. The Morrill Act of 1862 establishing the system of land-grant colleges together with the economic expansion following the Civil War led to a period of rapid increase in both institutions and enrollments. Many of the new colleges were the result of denominational competition. The founders were concerned to protect and to propagate the true faith. Even where religious belief did not constitute a factor, as with the state institutions, trustees maintained a stern and pervasive control over policies, personnel, and practices.[1]

Growth in size, in the range of instruction and in the problems of management created a need for more administration than busy trustees had time or talent to provide. The end of the nineteenth and the beginning of the twentieth centuries were an era of great university presidents—Eliot at Harvard, White at Cornell, Gilman at Johns Hopkins, Harper at Chicago, Jordan at Stanford, and many others. Like the great captains of industry, they seized power and ruled with autocratic authority. Trustees were content to take a back seat.

At the same time responsibility for internal management was becoming more decentralized. As divisions and departments multiplied, presidents could not maintain supervision over all aspects of university life. Just as the trustees had delegated authority to the presidents, so the presidents delegated authority over curriculum, contents of courses, academic requirements and standards, even the selection of new colleagues to the faculty. The founding of the American Association of University Professors in 1915 brought

1. In Governance of Higher Education we learn: "The first delegation of authority by the board to the president in the history of the University of California came in 1891 when the president was permitted to hire a janitor, provided he reported his action promptly to the board" (Carnegie Commission, 1973, p. 31).

into the open faculty concern for partnership in governance. Full recognition of the faculty's role came slowly and unevenly, but the extent to which faculty control over academic decisions has been dominant in this century is dramatically highlighted in the now classic Ruml/Morrison challenge entitled *Memo to a College Trustee*. As far back as 1959 they could say: "The Trustees, therefore, must take back from the faculty *as a body* its present authority over the design and administration of the curriculum" (Ruml, 1959, p.13).

The Classic Model

The pattern of governance which evolved in the nineteenth and early twentieth centuries did not always work well, and both the machinery and method of working varied with the type of institution. The regents of state universities arrived at their position by different routes from those of the trustees of private colleges. They had different obligations and were held responsible in different ways. Yet the main features of the traditional model are readily recognizable—a model that directed and managed the growth of what was probably in size and complexity the most extraordinary system of higher education in the world.

The classic model was a pyramid with the president at the apex, other administrative officers and the faculty lower down, and students at the bottom. Over and above this pyramid floated the board of trustees with complete legal authority, but with decreasing actual control. In its purest form the president, clothed with the authority of the board, ran the institution. He (rarely a she in those days) fashioned the budget, set the salaries, assigned office space, and maintained law and order among the students. Faculty concentrated on teaching, a few managing to squeeze out some time and energy for research and writing. Students were accepted on sufferance and were expected to defer to faculty judgment on what they needed to learn.

Even before World War II the hierarchical lines of authority were gradually being obliterated, in fact if not in theory, by the multiplication of departments and schools, by the diffusion of decision-making, and by steady faculty pressure for a more central role. Nevertheless, what made it work was *consensus*—consensus about goals, methods, roles, authority, and values. The consensus was never perfect, and toward the end of the era culminating in World War II it was growing perilously thin.

It functioned in different ways on different campuses. The greater the prestige of the institution, the more the faculty dominated the major areas of policy. Among black colleges the pattern of dominant presidents has tended to persist. Among community colleges, latecomers to the educational scene, governing boards typically exercise more authority in policy determination and even in actual administration.

And yet, in spite of differences in origin, in structure, in behavior, there was a sense of common enterprise. Colleges and universities had been founded to conserve, transmit, and create knowledge. The structures within which these functions were pursued resembled one another. The participation of faculty along with administration and governing boards was recognized as legitimate and constructive. Governance was, in a highly flexible sense of the term, collegial.

Forces of Disruption

Forces at work within our society since World War II have so altered this traditional pattern of higher education that colleges and universities are confused about their mission, uncertain of their methods, and bewildered by conflicting pressures both from within and from without. What will the consequences be? Will we in due course, after working our way through the thicket of uncertainties and confusions, return to the familiar model? Some students of governance believe that the traditional system cannot survive. "But social trends will probably undermine even the limited collegial influence that existed. Frankly, it seems that collegial governance is for the most part dead. We may not think it should be, but we definitely think it is" (Baldridge, 1978, p.224). Let us take a look at some of the "acids of modernity," to use Walter Lippmann's phrase, which are eroding the old pattern.

Increase in enrollments. The G.I. Bill unleashed a torrent, swelled by subsequent student aid legislation. In the last year before World War II, 1.5 million students were enrolled in American colleges and universities. By 1960 the figure had reached 3.6 million; by 1970, 8.6 million; and by 1980, 12.1 million. Nothing like it had ever been seen. The greatest expansion in 350 years of higher education had shattered the conventional academic mold. The new students coming from every social class and economic background presented a diversity of expectations and needs which required the diversification of post-secondary education. A populist mood demanded equal treatment for everyone, open admissions, courses and standards to meet every demand. What was once a privilege has now become a right.

Community colleges. In the last 50 years two-year colleges have nearly tripled in number, public community colleges accounting for most of the increase. The intent, largely though not entirely achieved, has been to make postsecondary facilities available to anyone wishing to go on from high school or to any older person ambitious enough to seek self-improvement. The community college movement has relieved many pressures on the older four-year institutions; but in the course of doing so, it has developed its own problems of governance in addition to those plaguing all postsecondary education.

Statewide systems. In the last 20 years, every state has established some sort of coordinating commission with responsibility to review and plan for the needs of postsecondary education within the state. In all but a few states there are now one or more statewide governing boards exercising control over several campuses (in New York 74 units!). Such boards represent an attempt to rationalize the competing and often overlapping programs of state institutions, and in the face of rapidly rising costs to hold the various colleges and universities accountable.

The logic seems impeccable. Increased demands for state services, of which education is usually the most costly, lead to increased state taxes, and these in turn lead to public resistance and the demand that education be made more efficient or at least that its efficiency be guaranteed by state control. Accountability is presented as a reasonable safeguard. Yet it can end by destroying the autonomy of the institution.

Politicization. Statewide governing boards are widely perceived as posing a threat to the autonomy of individual institutions accustomed to managing their own affairs. In addition, the governor's office, the budget director, the educational committees of the state legislature in turn present ever-present dangers to statewide boards. Created to serve as a buffer between the institutions and direct political influence, the statewide boards are nevertheless vulnerable to political manipulation and control. This is one form of politicization. The other form springs from within the campus. It was most evident in the sixties with student demands for participatory democracy and threats of direct action to gain their ends.

Many younger faculty sided with the students, creating factionalism within the faculty. The old mode of consensus began giving way to confrontation. Demands that the college or university be used as an instrument for social or political reform created further strains. While the disruption of the sixties has receded, its scars remain. Campuses are no longer the same. One legacy is the strong "consumer" attitude. The increasing resort to law courts to settle internal academic disputes is evidence of the breakdown of the older goals and values. Finally, there is the rise of collective bargaining by faculty—the substitution of formal adversarial relations for the more informal consensus achieved through a sense of common purpose and shared community.

Federal support and intervention. The importance of federal aid is well demonstrated by the consternation caused by its cutback in the early eighties. Various restrictions, however, have been attached to federal support—affirmative action,

2. "There is currently a fad—perhaps a social movement—which is sweeping through postsecondary education. The movement is called 'consumerism'" (Stark, 1975).

equal opportunity in employment, in facilities for the handicapped, in support for women's as well as men's athletics. The spirit behind these requirements is commendable; the letter of their application leaves much to be desired. Here again the freedom of institutions to manage their own affairs is impaired or at least threatened.

From growth to decline. Higher education in the United States has been a growth industry. For 300 years it has grown, sometimes slowly and in the last three decades at an explosive rate. Now it faces a new prospect—at the best a steady state, at the worst a debilitating decline. The college age cohort will shrink for a decade, and no one knows how many will enroll on full- or part-time basis. The temper of the times is not likely to increase financial support from federal, state or private sources. Governance is tougher in lean years than in plenty. Retrenchment is hard. Competition grows fierce. The distant future may be very bright, but the intervening years, as Clark Kerr argues, may be rough (Kerr, 1975, 1979, also Carnegie Foundation, 1975).

Confusion of mission. This is the inevitable consequence of the social, economic, political, and educational forces tearing the educational establishment apart. "The gravest single problem facing American higher education," writes Lord Ashby, a friendly but astute English critic, "is this alarming disintegration of consensus about purpose. It is not just that the academic community cannot agree on technicalities of curricula, certification, and governance: it is a fundamental doubt about the legitimacy of universities as places insulated from society to pursue knowledge disengaged from its social implications" (Ashby, 1970, p. 104).

THE NEW ROLE FOR TRUSTEES

*As I see it, there is no other way that as few people
can raise the quality of the whole American society
as far and as fast as can trustees and directors of
our voluntary institutions, using the strength they
now have in the positions they now hold.*

Robert K. Greenleaf (1973)

12

In the light of the many disruptive forces listed in the preceding chapter, the members of the Carnegie Commission on Higher Education agree with the reluctant conclusion reached by Baldridge cited on page 52. "We believe," they write, "that it is unlikely that the old consensus will suffice for the future. A new situation exists both in the relation of the campus to society and on the campus itself" (1973, p.76). Elsewhere in their report they speak of "the need for independent and devoted boards of trustees to enhance the external independence and the internal equilibrium of the campus" (p.2).

In the face of multiple and sometimes conflicting purposes, of divided faculty loyalties, of competing student expectations, there is no other group than the trustees, both deeply concerned and yet above the fray, to insist on the clarification of mission, to monitor institutional progress, to protect the independence and integrity of the institution. Only strong boards which command public respect can effectively champion institutional autonomy. As higher education moves from governance by consensus to governance by conflict, the adjudicating role of trustees draws them more and more deeply into the principles and policies by which institutions function. A nation in social motion will not leave educational patterns at rest. "Any serious fundamental change in the intellectual outlook of human society," wrote Whitehead, "must necessarily be followed by an educational revolution" (1949).

The precise role of governing boards will vary from one type of institution to another, and each board will need to work out its own formula. The boards, for example, of church-related colleges and universities have special obligations to the sponsoring denominations. The regents of tax supported universities face demands for accountability from the general citizenry, from the governor, from the state legislature and from the state accounting office. The community college trustee must be responsive to the educational needs of the community and the educational demands, often predominantly vocational, of local citizens. The trustees of statewide systems, whether coordinating or governing, have a different assignment from the trustees or regents of individual institutions and to that extent must play a different role. It is further worth noting that the trustees of public institutions established by statute (and this is particularly true of community colleges) may exercise only those powers expressly assigned to them, whereas the trustees of private institutions may exercise all powers not expressly prohibited.

Not everyone views the past role of trustees with approval or their prospective role with confidence. In some academic circles it has been customary to denigrate trustees as either absentee landlords or not very bright busybodies. Early in the century that sardonic genius, Thorstein Veblen, epitomized the views of many of his colleagues:

Indeed, except for a stubborn prejudice to the contrary, the fact should readily be seen that the boards are of no material use in any connection; their sole effectual function being to interfere with the academic management in matters that are not of the nature of business and that lie outside their competence and outside the range of their habitual interest. The governing boards—trustees, regents, cu-

14

rators, fellows, whatever their style and title —are an aimless survival from the days of clerical rule when they were presumably of some effect in enforcing conformity to ortho-dox opinions and observances, among the academic staff (Veblen, 1957, p. 48).

And more recently Henry G. Manne, Distin-guished Professor of Law at the University of Miami, said in an address:

Instead of being directed by trustees, the modern private university has become "de-mocratized," with an almost total loss of trus-tees' control over the three principal ingredi-ents of university policy—student admissions, faculty hiring and curriculum…. This is a rather bleak forecast for the future of boards of trustees of universities but, in fact, that group seems well on its way to near-impotence (Manne, 1972).

In contrast to these views it is encouraging to read the comment of a contemporary historian of educational organization and governance, Pro-fessor E.D. Duryea of SUNY Buffalo:

Little attention is given, unfortunately, to the uniquely significant role of the governing board in this country as the agency that both has protected internal autonomy and intel-lectual freedom and has served as a force to keep institutions relevant to the general society (Duryea, 1973, p. 22).

One of the purposes of this study is to focus at-tention on "the uniquely significant role of the governing board." It can be summed up in three propositions: first, that the traditional model of governance is inadequate to the circumstances of the present and future; second, that a period of

confusion and uncertainty is a time of great opportunity since the pattern of the future can be
deliberately shaped; and third, that governing
boards will need to play a major role in shaping
the destiny of higher education. It is the thesis of
this essay that the governing boards of higher education, if they are prepared to respond to current
opportunities, will play a more important role in
the years ahead than at any time in this century.

What, then, are the responsibilities which they
must assume in order to play their proper role?
Chapter 3 outlines in some detail the responsibilities of trustees as individuals. At first blush
the list looks formidable, but it could easily be
reduced in number. For purposes of exposition
and explanation it is preferable to see how each
responsibility is distinct from yet related to the
others. Chapter 4 deals with their responsibilities
as members of governing boards — their collective
responsibilities. All trustees need to keep in
mind that, while they have responsibilities as
individuals, they have no authority save as members of a board.

THE RESPONSIBILITIES OF TRUSTEES

*In summary, then, my concept of trusteeship is to
make Cornell eminently worthy of survival and
to assure that she does, in fact, survive.*

Robert L. Sproull, Trustee

18

No one should enter into trusteeship lightly. It is an honor to be invited to serve on a college or university board and service can be very rewarding. But it is a tough assignment, requiring a genuine commitment of time, intelligence, and hard work. This chapter is an attempt to identify and describe the major reponsibilities involved.

1. To Maintain the Integrity of the Trust

Trustees may come and go, but the boards of which they are members provide the continuity which every institution needs. They provide the stability over time which is one of the conditions for preserving integrity. These three—continuity, stability, and above all integrity—are the trust which trustees must protect.

Every college and university was founded for a particular purpose or set of purposes. It had its mission—to bring up young people in the proper faith, for example, or to provide opportunities for self-development and useful training at public expense. Trustees are the guardians of the mission, as originally set forth or later modified under pressure of different conditions. They must make sure that the institution's programs conform to its stated purpose and that funds are spent in accordance with the terms under which they are accepted.

The turbulent conditions of the past two decades produced many changes in academic programs, practices and structures, not all of which were beneficial. The static or declining enrollments of the '80s together with sharp restrictions on available funds will put further pressure on postsecondary education. The temptations will be great to inflate promises of educational advantage, to scrounge up programs of dubious value inconsistent with the historical character of the institution, to jeopardize the future by deferring maintenance or consuming capital assets in current expenditures.

To be sure, the present situation offers opportunities as well as dangers. The current call for market strategies, for example, can lead to distinct improvements in recruitment policies; it can also end up in hucksterism (Stark, 1975). It is the responsibility of trustees to make certain that long-term values are not sacrificed for short-term gains, and that existing assets are not lost or abandoned through negligence.[1]

2. To Appoint the President

Hugh Calkins, Fellow of Harvard, begins his proposal, "A Plan for Survival," with the statement: "Nathan M. Pusey used to say that the function of a member of the Harvard Corporation was to see that the university was properly staffed and that the bills were paid" (*AGB Reports*, Jan/Feb. 1975). The proper staffing of a college or university begins with the president.

The president is—or ought to be—the most important single individual connected with the institution. Important, first, because he or she is the primary agent of the board, to whom the board delegates its authority to manage or administer the institution in accordance with policies approved by the board. That makes the president powerful. Important, second, because in the future as in the past the strongest, the best, the most distinctive colleges and universities result from the educational leadership of men and women with vision and conviction. This makes the president

1. When is it the duty of trustees to close a college? The not inconsiderable number which have closed their doors in the past few years suggests that there are valid reasons, chiefly financial, for ending the trust. In the Wilson College case, however, the trustees were enjoined from closing the college by the Orphans Court judge in Chambersburg, Pa. He ruled that the trustees had been derelict in fulfilling their responsibilities and that the college was not in the desperate financial condition they claimed. He ordered a reorganization of the board and the continuation of the college. In short, the trustees had failed to meet their primary responsibility as trustees. See AGB Reports, July/Aug. 1980, for three articles which review the situation in some detail. In the same year, 1979, the New York state board of regents removed the trustees of Mannes College of Music who were seeking to merge it with the Manhattan School of Music on grounds that "the Mannes College board of trustees has, during the past year, demonstrated with respect to certain critical matters a collective neglect of duty which is appalling." The regents appointed a new board of trustees. See The Chronicle of Higher Education, Nov. 5, 1979.

2. See Joseph F. Kauffman, The
Selection of College and University
Presidents, Association of
American Colleges 1974; John W.
Nason, Presidential Search,
Association of Governing Boards,
1979; and for a shorter treatment.
Chapter 8 "Selecting the Chief
Executive" in Richard T. Ingram
(Ed.): Handbook of College and
University Trusteeship,
Jossey-Bass 1980.

influential and effective. It follows that the selection and appointment of the president (together with the support and supervision discussed in the next section) are the most important responsibilities of trustees.

With an able president who understands the job, most other problems are solvable. With a poor president even good institutions are in for trouble. This is not the place to explore the best procedures for finding and appointing the president.[2] It is a tricky and complex job involving an analysis of institutional needs and the participation of faculty, students, and others in the search and preliminary screening processes.

The chief administrative officers should serve at the discretion of and be responsible to the president. None should report independently to the board. This does not mean that there should not be direct communication between the financial vice president or a dean and the board or board committees. It does mean that the board which feels it must set a watchdog over the president would be wiser to seek a new president. Nor does it mean that the president should avoid discussing the administrative team with the trustees and getting their advice on the right people and the best organization. The board, however, should act through the president.

3. To Make Certain that the Institution Is Well Managed

The appointment of the president is the first and most important step. Unfortunately too many boards in the past—and some today—stop there. Trustees should not meddle in management, but they need to be sure that the management is good.

The assessment of the administration can be informal or formal, continuous or periodic, focused on the president's office or on the total governance of the institution. In times past presidents held indefinite appointments or annual appointments which were automatically renewed each year. Their actions and decisions were, and indeed still are, constantly scrutinized by faculty, students, staff, trustees, alumni, the general public; if presidents of state institutions, by various state officials and the hierarchy of the statewide system; if heading church-related colleges, by members of the supporting religious order or denomination. Alert and conscientious boards provide quiet counseling of a kind to enhance the president's effectiveness. It is all too easy, however, to leave matters alone, to hope that in time problems will solve themselves, and then to be faced with a crisis which requires drastic action.

The trend in recent years has been to give presidents term appointments and to make a conscious, specific and therefore more formal assessment of their stewardship before renewing the appointment. The advocates of this procedure point out that it gives the president a definite contract, that it eliminates some of the pressures between appointments, that it treats the president very much as others are treated, and provides directions for the institution's future as well as directives for the president.

There are, however, disadvantages in this system, and many boards and presidents may prefer a more flexible arrangement. However it is played, it is important that both president and board agree on the criteria of satisfactory performance, preferably when the president is first appointed.

3. For a more detailed discussion of the pros and cons of presidential evaluation see in the Handbook already cited Chapter 19, "Reviewing Presidential Leadership," by Barry Munitz, who is probably the best informed and most experienced commentator on this subject. Also John W. Nason: Presidential Assessment, Association of Governing Boards 1980. Joseph F. Kauffman: At the Pleasure of the Board, American Council on Education 1980, presents a sensitive and highly readable picture of the complexity of the contemporary college and university president's job.

Are board policies being faithfully carried out? Is the institution growing stronger or weaker? Are the institutional goals clear, and is the president providing the time and talents necessary to achieve those goals? Where performance is unsatisfactory and shows little likelihood of improvement, trustees should reach the decision to change the administration before a crisis blows up in their faces. A quietly arranged departure is kinder to the individual and far better for the institution[3]

The trustees' responsibility for seeing that the college or university is well managed cannot be limited to the president's office, even though the president is the agent through whom their decisions and concerns are channeled. How good are the chief's principal lieutenants? How well do they work together? The president may not see clearly weaknesses in the performance of others. He or she may be too tender or too loyal to take proper action without encouragement or insistence from the board. Failure to achieve certain goals may be due to faculty opposition, objections by members of a religious group or politics in the state capitol. In such cases an assessment of the whole picture might well result in strong board support of the president's position.

This leads to one final aspect of the trustees' responsibility for oversight of the general operations of the institution. Under the best of circumstances the modern college president's job is not easy. It can be very satisfying, but it is full of frustrations. The governance of a college or university is one of shared authority and power. Cohen and March (1974) describe the contemporary college as organized anarchy. If the president takes no clear stand on important issues, he or she will be condemned as unimaginative or rudderless. Any decisive stand will be praised by those who favor it, condemned by those on the board who are opposed.

These built-in pressures and conflicts become in time emotionally exhausting. A wise board will watch their president, providing aid and comfort. They will provide support when support is appropriate. They will see that he or she gets adequate relief from pressure, that provision is made for personal professional interests, that areas where the president is less competent are compensated for by other administrative arrangements. "Given the substantial investment a governing board makes in finding a president," writes Kauffman, "it is simply good management for the board to conserve this important resource. Leadership is a scarce and precious asset that should not be taken for granted" (p.61).

4. To Approve the Budget

Having explored in the last two sections the first half of the Pusey formula for trustees, let us now examine the second half, namely, to see that the bills are paid. This will be increasingly difficult in the decade ahead.

When the budget becomes unbalanced, either income must be increased or expenditures decreased—or both. Significant increases in income —higher tuition, larger student body, a big-time sports program, joint research and development with industry, fund raising campaigns—involve board approval and participation.

In cutting costs, the president and his or her administrative staff can whittle down expenses bit by bit, but sooner or later drastic surgery is

24

needed—the elimination of an entire department or school or institute, the closing of a peripheral campus, substantial reduction of faculty including some on tenure—and once again board approval and support are needed.

In the long run it is the responsibility of the trustees to make certain that income matches outgo, that resources are sufficient to pay for programs, and that future financial health is not sacrificed to current demands. Short-term deficits may be preferable to the long-term damage resulting from drastic curtailment in personnel and programs, but trustees must be satisfied that bank loans or temporary drafts on capital funds to pay current bills will ultimately be restored by improvement in income. In the public sector trustees or regents rarely have this option, for state authorities usually require that the budget be balanced and with increasing frequency specify where cuts must be made.

To exercise financial responsibility trustees must understand what various financial statements are telling them. The concept of fund accounting widely used by college and university accountants is relatively simple, but it will require some concentrated time and attention from those trustees who are not familiar with it and who do not move easily and naturally in a world of figures. The Association of Governing Boards and the National Association of College and University Business Officers in a joint effort (1979) produced a handbook on the subject, *Financial Responsibilities of Governing Boards of Colleges and Universities*, which every trustee could study with profit. Unfortunately there still remain confusion and disagreement on how much financial information trustees need to have. Some — members of the financial committee, for example — will want more than others. Trustees should insist, as John W. Pocock argues in his excellent chapter, "Reporting Finances," in the *Handbook of College and University Trusteeship* already referred to, that they get accurate information in financial reports which are revealing and intelligible. Having received such information, trustees are under obligation to make whatever decisions are required for the financial solvency of the institution.

This is an obligation of *all trustees*. The newer and less experienced may defer to the judgment of those believed to be expert in seeing through figures, but they may not abdicate. They share a full and equal responsibility for the financial health of their institution.

5. To Raise Money

Balancing the budget by increasing income is far pleasanter than by cutting expenses. It is the responsibility of every trustee, of public as well as of private institutions, to increase the flow of new money from private gifts or from public appropriations or from both.

Their first obligation is to ensure that a sound program of fund raising is established. This will include distinctions between annual campaigns for operating income and periodic capital campaigns, between various sources of funds such as state and federal appropriations, private gifts from individuals, corporations, foundations, clear statements of need, adequate staffing, and orderly procedures of soliciting and reporting. In Chapter 14 of the *Handbook of College and University Trusteeship*, Radock and Jacobson provide a masterly summary of the scope and character of such a program, and the publications in their list of suggested readings provide a wealth of detail.

The second obligation of trustees is to participate. This is one area where trustees must become directly involved. They participate by their own giving and by their effectiveness in asking others to give. Without strong trustee leadership no capital campaign is likely to succeed, and the board which lacks individuals of ample means and generous motivation will have a hard time. Trustees with modest financial resources should contribute modestly, but contribute they must. No campaign should start without the 100 percent participation of the entire board. No trustee can reasonably ask others to give unless he or she has given.

Asking others is the second half of participation. No one, not even the president, is in as good a position to ask for support as the trustees, whose position gives them a special perspective, who are clearly not self-seeking, and whose commitment to the institution is seen as testimony to its worth. Even the timid who are reluctant to solicit should take their courage and their convictions in hand. One who is truly convinced that the college or university is worth supporting, should not find it all that difficult to ask others for support. If one is not that convinced, then one ought not to be on the board.[4] The trustees of public colleges and universities may feel less keenly the pressure of fund raising, but more and more public institutions are supplementing their appropriations with private funds, and public trustees are behaving like their private counterparts.

Every year, or every other year, there is a struggle in state capitols over the appropriations for

4. This may seem a harsh judgment, but the alternative looks very much like a cop-out. One possible exception is the judge who avoids any action that might seem to jeopardize his or her objectivity. Another could be the political figure who is fearful that he or she would be committed to returning some future favor.

postsecondary education. In the competition for limited funds, trustees and regents can and should be spokesmen for their institutions. Where they are members of the governing board of a single institution, they should be concerned that it gets its fair share of the money available. Where they are members of a statewide board, they must be advocates of the educational needs of the citizens of the state. Where they are trustees or directors of a community college, they must be prepared to argue their case before county boards or local agencies. Increasingly, the trustees of independent colleges and universities, almost all of which now accept public support in one way or another, must get into the act.

That act has two aspects or phases. One is lobbying. This is clearly more important for trustees of public institutions, for without state or local appropriations, state and community colleges could not exist; but both public and private institutions are dependent in part on federal funds. Representation of institutional interests and needs is vital at both state and federal levels. By virtue of their position and connections trustees can be very influential, particularly if they go about it in an organized and intelligent way.[5]

The second aspect centers on a concern for public policy. Changes in tax laws increase or diminish incentives to charitable giving. The President proposes and the Congress debates each year a federal budget, the terms of which affect colleges and universities across the country through research and development grants, financial aid to students, and other programs. In addition, colleges and universities are affected by government policies in employment, interest

5. In "How to Play the State Capitol Game" in AGB Reports, Sept./Oct. 1980, Daniel Angell, president of Imperial Valley College in California and formerly a member of the Michigan House of Representatives, provides blunt and useful advice on how to work with state legislators.

6. Robert M. Hyde, vice president of the Association of Independent Colleges and Universities in Massachusetts, argues the case trenchantly in "Why Don't Trustees Discuss Government?" in AGB Reports, Jan./Feb. 1977. Using an imaginary Foster College as an example he deplores the shortsightedness of the trustees who fail to be on guard against federal and state actions potentially inimical to Foster's welfare. "That is unfortunate," he writes, "for the future of the Fosters of this land — indeed, for the rich diversity which independent institutions bring to American higher education — depends almost entirely upon the outcome of public policy issues which will be decided in Washington and in state capitals during the next eight to ten years."

rates, health, and other areas not generally associated with education. Trustees need to consider, and if possible to influence, these developments. The Association of Governing Boards has recently recognized the importance of this area by establishing an office of public policy. The trustees of state colleges and universities have gone farthest in this field. Independent college trustees have done the least. It is a responsibility which all must share.[6]

6. To Manage the Endowment

Most private institutions and an increasing number of public universities have endowments and/or capital funds available for investment. Harvard leads the procession with an endowment in excess of $1.5 billion, and the University of Texas is not far behind. In 1980, there were 36 institutions with endowments above $100 million and, of these, five were public universities. Whether endowed or not, all institutions, public and private, have various temporary fund balances on hand. Prudent management calls for the investment of these funds on a short-term basis. Thus all trustees, and not merely those favored with large endowments, have a responsibility for the wise investment of available assets.

The problems of modern investment are such that most boards employ professional investment counsel to advise on the character of the investments and to handle the practical details. But the trustees as a whole, acting to be sure on the recommendations of a finance or investment committee, must approve the policies and conditions which provide the instructions to the professional counsel. Should funds be invested for high annual returns or for long-term gains? What ratio of equities to fixed-income securities? To what extent will the trustees invest in real estate, oil wells or relatively high risk ventures?

Another and troubling dimension stems from the competing claims of present versus future needs. In recent years under the heavy pressure for current income many non-profit organizations, colleges and universities among them, have turned to the concept of the total yield of their invested funds—i.e. dividends, interest, royalties, rents and capital gains—as a way of increasing current revenue. After all, it is argued, would not the college be better off by investing in a stock that paid no dividend but showed a steady 10 percent appreciation in value than by buying some security that paid a regular 5 percent dividend (or interest) and remained at a constant market value? Since the trustees must set each year the return on endowment to be made available for the operations of the institution, many now take into account capital appreciation as well as dividends and interest in setting that rate. In periods of inflation, however, some provision needs to be made to increase endowment to provide income with equivalent purchasing power in future years. How much of the capital gains should be salted away for meeting future expenses? Present needs have an urgency which is hard to ignore. The trustees' responsibility is to weigh the future against the present in order to maintain the integrity of the institution over the long run.

7. To Assure Adequate Physical Facilities

Colleges and universities need "a local habitation and a name." Even a "university without walls" requires an office and equipment. As part of their responsibility for the safekeeping of the institution's capital assets, trustees have traditionally exercised particular concern for the acquisition and preservation of buildings and grounds. Perhaps because the early presidents of American colleges and universities, chiefly ministers, were presumed to be inexperienced in practical matters, perhaps because most trustees felt more at home with the physical than the intellectual aspects of their institutions, trustees became directly involved in questions of plant management. Times and conditions have changed, and neither argument for direct trustee involvement is valid today.

Nevertheless, there are certain policy decisions for which the trustees are ultimately responsible. Is there a master plan for the campus? Is it consistent with the educational goals and programs of the institution? Is it realistic in terms of prospective enrollments and sources of funds? Does it have a measure of flexibility to accommodate changing needs and programs? The data on which intelligent answers can be based must come from faculty and administration. The answers themselves must have the stamp of board approval.

Trustees have a special responsibility for future generations of students. The same might be said for administrative officers, but they, like the faculty, are deeply concerned with the present generation. That concern, as we have noted, will sometimes result in favoring the present at the expense of the future. When the budget is tight, proper maintenance of buildings and grounds can be skimped. Human expenditures seem always more important than physical expenditures. Deferred maintenance, however, must sooner or later be made up, and the longer the delay, the higher the cost. The renewal and replacement of buildings and equipment are essential *at some level* to the continued existence and operation of the institution. As custodians of the trust, the trustees must decide on the level.[7]

8. To Oversee the Educational Program

For most of this century the conventional wisdom, shared by trustees as well as by faculty and administration, assigned to trustees responsibility for institutional property and finances and to the faculty responsibility for the academic program.[8] The fact that this division of labor worked as well as it did is something of a testimonial to the vitality of American higher education and to the tolerance and understanding exhibited by both parties. For clearly the distinction makes no sense. In safeguarding the mission and approving the goals trustees are determining the educational character of the institution. In approving the budget they are setting academic priorities. Their oversight of physical resources is predicated on the clientele served and the programs offered.[9]

No one has said it any better than that wise trustee (Carleton, Chicago, Harvard) and successful businessman and lawyer, Laird Bell:

Furthermore, the trustees cannot properly abdicate all concern with educational matters. Logically the trustees as the controlling body have the right—and in fact the duty—to determine what kind of education shall be offered. As custodians of the property and funds they are bound to see that they are devoted to the purposes for which they were given. They are free (subject to the terms of

7. In a recently published study, Hang-Gliding or Looking for an Updraft (1981), Hans Jenny and associates analyze this aspect of college and university finance. They emphasize the responsibility of trustees to safeguard future generations of students by planning for new capital equipment and renovation and replacement of old equipment and facilities, calling this "the capital margin."

8. Note the finding in a 1969 survey by the Carnegie Commission on Higher Education to the effect that 45% of 60,000 faculty polled agreed strongly or with reservations with the statement that "Trustees' only responsibility should be to raise money and gain community support" (Carnegie Commission, 1973, p. 90). The members of the Commission disagree (p. 33).

9. In a perceptive chapter "Managing Resources" in the Handbook Charles A. Nelson, a principal of Peat, Marwick, Mitchell and chairman of the board of visitors and governors of St. John's College, Annapolis, concludes his analysis with the comment: "Our main concern here is to emphasize that resources cannot be managed, whether by the administration or by the trustees, except by reference to a purpose or set of purposes—

32

10. "From the Trustees' Corner,"
address to the Institute for College
and University Administrators
(Harvard University, June 1956)
Association of American Colleges,
Bulletin, Vo.42, No.3, p.354.

their charter and endowments of course) to determine whether the institution shall be a liberal arts college, a technical school, a professional school or a teachers college, whether new projects shall be undertaken, new schools or institutes created, existing ones liquidated, and so on. They also can and should have much influence in what might be called the tone of the institution. But once overall policy is decided it ought to be true that the educational experts should determine how the policy is to be implemented.[10]

How can trustees best meet their responsibility for oversight of the educational program? By constantly asking questions. To what extent is the university living up to its stated mission? Is this new program or department or institute consistent with our long term goals? What old programs are expendable if new ones are to be added? And in a climate of retrenchment, what programs should be cut back, what programs sustained? What kind of student is the institution attracting? What are the chief student complaints? What are the major faculty concerns? How do we compare with similar institutions? If a public institution, how do we rate within the state system? If a community college, what evidence have we that we are serving the community in ways which will insure continued support?

What are the warning signals to which everyone should be alert? A drop in enrollment, a change in the composition of the student body, a decline in the success of seniors in getting into the graduate or professional schools, sudden changes in budget allocations, marked deviation in comparative statistics. The list is endless.

This responsibility applies to the trustee or regent of statewide and multicampus systems as much as to single institution boards. As we shall note in the concluding section of this chapter, the trustees of such systems have specially complicated and delicate tasks in approving programs consonant with the educational needs of the citizens on the one hand and with the competing demands for public funds on the other.

Two cautions are in order before ending this discussion. The first was amusingly stated by Charles A. Coolidge at a time when he was Senior Fellow of the Harvard Corporation. After reviewing the major obligations of a Fellow he concludes with the admonition: DON'T MEDDLE.[11] Laird Bell said it in another way. Trustees should approve educational policy; they should not interfere with the curriculum or with the ways in which policy is translated into action. That is the job of the faculty. Second, while the trustees have the final say, they should rely heavily on the recommendations of the president and the faculty. Presidents are professional educators (or should be). Their entire professional activity centers on the problems of education in general and of their institution in particular. They can be wrong, sometimes tragically wrong. Their recommendations should not be rubber-stamped, for even the best will sometimes make poor judgments. But trustees should assume until evidence proves otherwise that the presidents' views are sound and deserve support.

9. To Approve Long Range Plans

Planning is time-consuming work. If done well, it is comprehensive. If comprehensive, it involves

11. Charles A. Coolidge: "How To Be a Good Fellow" (1956).

the collection and digestion of a considerable amount of data—data on prospective enrollments, on faculty salary trends, on operating costs for plant and services, on projections of likely outside support in gifts or grants or appropriations, on changes in the national economy and in demands for services. Harassed by daily decisions and constant demands on his or her time, the president is tempted to put off structuring an uncertain future in favor of shoring up a none-too-steady present.

This is where the trustees come into the picture. They cannot make long range plans, but they can insist that the plans be made. Furthermore, they can insist that the plans be comprehensive, thorough and realistic. Paradoxically, the more uncertain the future and therefore the more difficult to plan for it, the more important the long range plans become. A few fortunate institutions may feel confident enough to be content with a single set of projections. Most colleges and universities will end up with a series of scenarios based on a series of different assumptions.

Standing outside the institution and involved in their own business and professional activities, trustees can take a detached view of the academic scene. They are less likely to lose sight of the educational forest by being lost among academic trees. They can ask the tough questions the answers to which may well be the price of survival.

10. To Serve as Bridge and Buffer Between Campus and Community

Bridge and buffer are contrary functions, for one facilitates movement and exchange while the other blocks them. At different times and in different contexts, however, trustees must perform both functions.

The last section ended with emphasis on the contribution trustees can make to an institution's long range plans. As laymen involved with the concerns and issues of the surrounding society, they are in a position to interpret the needs of that society to the campus community and to suggest the future directions which it will take. Colleges far more than universities, especially the multi-versities (to use Clark Kerr's now familiar term), tend to be self-centered and all too often self-satisfied communities existing apart from the out-side "real" world. They become ingrown, insu-lated (less now than formerly) from outside forces. But university as well as college communities are naturally protective of their traditional values and practices, conservative about their own profes-sion (no matter how radical in their critique of others), slow to change.

Trustees are, or ought to be, the antennae of their institution, relaying back what the surround-ing world is like. Their responsibility is to en-courage constructive change. They should not try to engineer such change; that is the task of faculty and administration. At the very least their respon-sibility is to challenge the status quo; at best it is to transmit the needs and temper of society and to suggest the direction which programs might take.[12] The trustees of church-related colleges may need to remind faculty and administration of the views and expectations of the supporting denom-ination or to interpret currents of thought which might affect the stance of the institution. The mandate assigned to members of statewide gov-erning or coordinating boards includes not only

12. A vigorous statement on this subject, and indeed on the role of trustees in general, is to be found in Beardsley Ruml and Donald Morrison: Memo to a College Trustee (McGraw-Hill, 1959). In the final chapter of The Board of Trustees of the Private Liberal Arts College, Miriam Wood makes some trenchant comments on the responsibility of trustees for the public interest. Institutional advantage may or may not be consistent with the public good. What policies should the college or university pursue if there is a conflict? This raises some of the larger issues to which trustees ought properly to address themselves.

attention to the current needs of the citizens of the state, but to future needs as well.

The traffic in ideas should also move across the bridge in the opposite direction. The personal standing of the trustee and his or her willingness to contribute time and service to the institution say much to the community about the value of the college or university. In talks with state or local officials, with members of a church group, with the general public, the trustee's voice can be the most persuasive in informing others about the programs of the institution.

At this point the roles of bridge and buffer tend to merge. By their very nature colleges and universities are seats of controversy. The free flow of ideas on the one hand and the uninhibited behavior of student bodies on the other will shock most of the people some of the time and some of the people most of the time. Trustees must be prepared to explain why freedom of research, of thought, and of teaching are basic to our form of society. They must be ready to refute the ugly rumors which have no basis in fact. They must, as we noted in an earlier section, roll up their sleeves and persuade state legislators and private donors that the university or the college deserves their support.

The dual role of bridge and buffer can easily become a paradoxical one for the trustees or regents of state colleges and universities. In a perceptive chapter on the "Conflicting Responsibilities of Governing Boards," Perkins (1973) drives home the dilemma. "But how does a regent act as an agent of the state and as a member of an autonomous organization at the same time? How does a regent conceive his role when he is ap-

pointed by the state to an office designed to pro-tect the institution from the state itself?" (pp.208-9). This goes to the heart of the problem of institutional autonomy discussed in the following section.

Trustees should work as persistently as possible to strengthen what they see as weaknesses in their institutions, to correct what are believed to be faults or errors. Those efforts should take place in the board room or the president's office, never in public. It can well be that a board will adopt policies with which some member does not agree. In such cases the individual must accept the majority decision and defend it, if necessary, in public; or, if the issue is so momentous that the trustee cannot do this in good faith, than he or she should resign.

11. To Preserve Institutional Autonomy

In defending the institution from outside interference, the trustee is protecting its integrity and independence. This has been one of the trustee's major responsibilities; and if there were no other reasons for a lay board, it could be justified on this ground alone. In two very perceptive articles, Martin Trow, professor of sociology at the University of California, Berkeley, discusses the distinction between the private and the public character of American higher education. The private life of colleges and universities consists of what happens in classrooms and laboratories, in teaching and research, in the development of individual potentialities and in the demands of scholarship. The public life centers around the committees and conferences, negotiations and decisions, resulting from society's demands for

38

more and better educational opportunities, for compensatory education for the handicapped or underprivileged, for increased services to industry and agriculture, for shifting training programs to accommodate long or short manpower supplies. The private functions are largely autonomous, made by faculty, students, librarians and deans. The public functions are largely dictated by outside forces.[13]

The freedom of the university to manage its internal affairs without outside interference has never been absolute, but it has been substantial. The nature of the educational enterprise requires a high degree of autonomy. The capacity for independent thought will not flourish under thought control. The university's function as a critic of society presupposes a certain independence from the society being criticized. With the support of understanding trustees, real progress has been made in institutional autonomy.

Some donors, to be sure, still insist on influencing economic or social policy, or try to do so, by putting improper conditions on their gifts. Some alumni groups or local booster clubs succeed in distorting the true nature of the university by forcing it to adopt a "big time" sports program or undermine its integrity by raising private purses for football coaches or basketball stars. But on the whole, this sort of outside pressure, among independent colleges and universities at least, has diminished. Even among the 700 church-related colleges and universities the sponsoring religious bodies are showing more understanding and restraint. In a recent study (1977) 93 percent of the Catholic colleges in this country indicated that they now had lay members on their boards of

13. "Reflections on the Transition from Mass to Universal Higher Education" in Daedalus, Vol 99, No.1 (Winter 1970). "The Public and Private Lives of Higher Education" in Daedalus, Vol 104, No.1 (Winter 1975)

trustees and an overwhelming majority were no longer under the control of the religious order or body which had founded them.[14]

During the '70s, a new threat to autonomy made itself felt. Increasing federal aid to higher education brought a variety of new federal regulations and restrictions—affirmative action, equal opportunity, equality in men's and women's sports programs, special provisions for the handicapped. These, and a host of others, were aimed at legislating a better society. They came, however, from outside. They had a kind of bureaucratic brutality and involved a stultifying amount of paperwork. They raised a hornet's nest of lawsuits. If federal support had become essential, some price had to be paid, but it became a new task of the trustees along with administrators to limit as much as possible the federal encroachment on the private life of higher education.

The trustees and regents of state universities and colleges encountered an even more dangerous threat—the growth of statewide systems of governing and coordinating boards. In many states the system board has supplanted the boards of the institutions composing the system. In others the individual boards remain, largely in an advisory capacity though sometimes with certain residual powers (such as determining voice in the selection of the president in the SUNY system). It may well be that individual governing boards of state universities and colleges are on their way to extinction.

The arguments for statewide systems will be discussed in the final section of this chapter in connection with the special responsibilities of the members of statewide boards. If this change

14. *Current Issues in Catholic Higher Education,* Published by the Association of Catholic Colleges and Universities, 1981. See also Robert Rue Parsonage, Ed.: Church Related Higher Education, Judson Press, Valley Forge, 1978.

in governance structure means the disappearance of effective individual boards, a heavy price will be paid. Nor is this the place to examine the weaknesses and dangers of the suppression of institutional initiative, the use of formulas instead of individual judgment, the tendency to homogenize rather than differentiate the quality of institutions, the inevitable costs and delays of bureaucracy, decisions by the not really informed, increased susceptibility to political control.[15]

One way is to encourage the continuation of individual boards wherever possible and with as much authority as possible. Recall the distinction made by Trow between the private and the public life of the university. The Carnegie Commission on Higher Education had something like this distinction in mind in its 1973 Report on *Governance of Higher Education*, saying that higher education needs to be largely self-governing with respect to its intellectual atmosphere (academic freedom), its academic procedures (curriculum) and its administration (financial and personnel decisions). Competition among state institutions can be wasteful and at the state capitol annoying, but it provides a strong impetus to distinction. It is heartening to hear former Governor Bowen of Indiana, a state with a statewide coordinating rather than governing board, say:

> *Regarding institutions, I think it crucial that they maintain a sense of distinctiveness and quality. They should not maintain their pre-occupation with size....Our institutions should be competing on the basis of excellence, not on the basis of overlapping programs and Services.* (AGB Reports, *Nov./Dec. 1979*)

15. See, for example, Enarson, "The Occasional Search for the Public Interest," AGB Reports, March/April 1975; Millett, "What, No Governing Board?" AGB Reports, Nov./Dec. 1975; Scarlett, "Why Presidents Don't Like State Boards," AGB Reports, Sept./Oct. 1980; Mumatz, "Memo to a Multicampus Trustee . . . From a Flagship CEO," AGB Reports, Sept./Oct. 1981.

Indiana is one of the states in which each institution of postsecondary education has its own governing board. Each, therefore, has a lay group concerned for the autonomy of the institution, a group that is prepared to support the kind of competition Governor Bowen recommends and presumably to serve in the role described by David Sweet, a president who has served under two state systems:

Now, it is my contention that the heart of education and the heart of teaching/learning, research and scholarship occurs at an institution. It doesn't occur in systems.... The difficulty of the Multiinstitutional single board system is that its colleges and universities are denied access to a caring board of lay persons who are committed solely to the institution and its development (AGB Reports, Jan./Feb. 1980).

12. To Serve as Court of Appeal

Since trustees possess final legal authority, there is no body other than the courts or the legislature which can legitimately challenge their decisions. Faculty, students or parents may protest the board's decisions and may argue for some different policy, but short of lobbying in the state capitol in the case of public institutions, or going to court in the case of public and private colleges and universities, they have no further redress.

Boards should insist on codes governing faculty appointment, promotion, tenure, leaves of absence and codes setting forth student rights, privileges, and obligations. These should have board approval and backing, should be clearly publicized, and should include provision for due process. Having done this, trustees should stay out of internal decisions and disputes until an appeal is made to their adjudication or until a case is filed in court. At that point the board must make certain that all proper procedures have been followed and then decide the issue or share in the college's defense. The trustees have a right to assume that a firm and intelligent administration proceeding in an orderly and fair manner will dispose of most disagreements at an early stage, but the recent history of academic litigation suggests that even the best managed institutions cannot be sure of avoiding unpleasant, unnecessary and costly confrontations.

13. To Be Informed

To be a good trustee an individual must, first of all, be interested in the college or university. There would be no point in volunteering time, effort and money if one were not. Second, the trustee must want to help, to be of service, to contribute to making the institution a stronger or better college or university. To do this the trustee must be willing to learn, to become informed. One assumes that trustees are intelligent; one expects them to become knowledgeable. Logically this responsibility might have been listed first, as it is a condition of the proper exercise of the other responsibilities. Its full significance, however, can be more easily grasped in the light of those responsibilities.

What do trustees need to know? To begin with, they need to understand the peculiar nature of an educational institution. It is unlike other organizations and institutions, functioning by its own ground rules, marching, as it were, to its own drummer. In the words of two economists quoted by Millett (1978): "University education, when examined through economists' eyes, assumes characteristics of a unique industry. This is because: (1) those who consume its product do not purchase it; (2) those who produce it do not sell it; and (3) those who finance it do not control it" (pp. 19-20).

Colleges and universities cannot be run like business enterprises, as many businessmen discover when they become trustees.[16] The rugged individualism of academic departments and schools, the shared authority with faculty, the limitations on presidential power, the principle of academic freedom—all these, so strange at first to those coming from a different world, need to be understood. It is encouraging to note in Hartnett's now classic study of the backgrounds and educational attitudes of trustees that top business executives understood better than businessmen in general that colleges could not be run like businesses. One assumes that they became business executives in part because they were sensitive to such differences.[17]

In the second place, trustees need to know as much as possible about the institution of which they are trustees—its history, mission and goals, programs, finances, physical assets, sources of students, qualitative status in the educational hierarchy, distinctive characteristics, major problems, future prospects. Some of this information will be found in the catalogue, the recent reports of the president, treasurer, vice presidents, provost and deans, in the bylaws, recent board minutes and in a manual (if it exists) outlining the structure and operations of the institution's gov-

16. For an amusing description of the shock of first exposure to the peculiarities of the academic world, see Chester L. Posey's "The Things I've Unlearned" in AGB Reports, Nov./Dec. 1979.

17. In 1967-68, Rodney T. Hartnett of the Educational Testing Service and Morton Rauh, vice president at Antioch College, undertook a survey of the trustees of over 500 colleges and universities. Replies were received from 5,000 trustees. Hartnett published the results in 1969 under the title, College and University Trustees. While now somewhat dated, it remains one of the most comprehensive and illuminating summaries of the nature of trustees by age, sex, profession, religion, income and attitude toward sensitive college and university policies.

ernance. Much of the information will need to be supplied by the president. Conversations with administrative officers, faculty, and students will provide different perspectives. Trustees should constantly ask why, why, why. The student newspaper and the alumni journal can be helpful. This is a large order, but the fact remains that a good trustee is an informed trustee.[18]

Finally, trustees need to be aware of the issues agitating higher education in general, particularly those which will have an impact on their institution. The trend of events becomes significant. In the not too distant past the civil rights movement, the appearance of black studies and of urban studies, the demise of *in loco parentis*, brought about significant changes in institutions across the country. A comparison of one's own institution with others is also illuminating. How do faculty salaries at institution X compare with those at similar institutions? Is the endowment yield, the number of applicants for admission, the percentage of the budget spent on library services better or worse than that at comparable institutions? What about long-term changes in the national scene? Does the current federal cutback in aid to students create a temporary or long-term problem for higher education? Will the desirability of some form of postsecondary education be seen in the years ahead by the general public as greater or less? No one can be certain of the answers, but the wisdom of trustees is important in developing working formulas.

The older stereotype of the trustee depicted him (rarely her) as an elderly businessman, banker or lawyer, successful, conservative, competent in financial matters, remote and largely ignorant

18. Part 5 of the *Rioni and Morrison Memo to a College Trustee* contains a useful summary of the areas in which trustees should be informed.

about academic affairs. The evidence suggests that there may have been some truth in this composite portrait, but less than the critics believed. Trustees have come a long way in the past quarter century, and faculty would do well to heed the words of one of the best, Atherton Bean, recipient of the first AGB Award for Distinguished Service in Trusteeship:

> I suggest that it is time for faculties and administrations to re-evaluate this situation in the light of the fact that they are dealing with a new breed of trustees. These trustees are almost all college-educated. A high percentage have advanced degrees. They are alive to various organizational styles. Most have traveled the world extensively. As mentioned earlier, they are continually subjected to the educative process in their own businesses and professions. Many of them are involved in the margins of scientific and social thought. I suggest the time has come not merely for the trustee to interest himself in the guts of the educational process but also for faculties to welcome that interest and advice (Bean, 1975).

Not every trustee will meet this high standard—not yet at least. Many, no doubt, under pressure of time and competing demands, give less time to informing themselves about their "trust" than is here suggested as desirable. More trustees, however, and more boards are proving themselves to be knowledgeable and thereby responsible.

The Special Problems of System Trustees

One of the remarkable phenomena in higher education in the last 20 years has been the growth

of multicampus and statewide systems of governance and coordination. The final report of the
Carnegie Council on Policy Studies in Higher
Education (1980) entitled *Three Thousand
Futures* states that in 1978, only 21 of the 141
member institutions of the National Association
of State Universities and Land-Grant Colleges, or
15 percent, still had their individual governing
boards. Eighty-five percent were part of statewide systems. In all, 164 multicampus boards
govern 886 institutions enrolling more than 50
percent of all students enrolled full time in postsecondary education.

Created in response to the need for a more
rational ordering of the educational resources of
a state, multicampus governing boards have
proved to be a mixed blessing. The transfer of
authority for major policy decisions to a systems
board has reduced the amount of institutional
infighting with state legislators over appropriations. It has facilitated statewide planning. It
seems to provide a higher degree of accountability for the expenditure of increasing amounts
of public money. It also gives both state legislatures and governors much greater control over
what has come to be the biggest area of state
expenditure.[19] While coordinating boards have
widely varying powers to deal with the publicly
supported institutions in their states, they do not
yet have mandatory authority over the private
institutions of the state (save in the case of the
Regents of the University of New York). Their
impact on the private sector can be seen in
recommendations for student grant-in-aid programs and for the expansion or contraction of
specific programs and facilities.

19. See John M. Lavine's article on
    "The Value of a Single System" in
    AGB Reports. January/February
    1980.

There is little prospect that the trend toward systems—whether governing or coordinating or both—will be reversed. Martin Trow argues in the articles referred to earlier in this chapter that the growth in the number of college-age young people attending colleges and universities led inevitably to heightened public concern over what happens on college and university campuses, over the penetration, in short, of the private life of the university by public factors. Section 11 of this chapter mentions some of the losses as well as gains in this development. To minimize the threats to institutional autonomy is the challenge to the statesmanship of statewide system trustees.

With multicampus and statewide systems being relatively new phenomena in our educational world, we are still in the process of discovering how system trustees can make their most useful contribution. They clearly share to some degree most of the responsibilities pertaining to their institutional brethren. What special obligations have they as system trustees? At least the following six must be undertaken.

1. **To make sure that citizens get the educational services they need.** The number of students enrolled in postsecondary education (quite apart from proprietary schools and the often extensive training programs within industry) has increased from 1.5 million in 1939-40, the last pre-World War II year, to 12.3 million 1981-82. The total budget for postsecondary education has grown to $152 billion. In some states the largest single appropriation is for higher education. This is big business. It affects the lives and the livelihood of a majority of the citizens of the state. Those citizens have a right to expect that some agency is

seeing to it that they get the services they need. The statewide systems are those agencies, and their trustees have the responsibility of setting statewide goals and programs.

2. **To allocate educational services among state institutions.** In the social pecking order the old normal schools have sought (and largely succeeded) in becoming state colleges with their wide diversity of programs; state colleges seek to become full-fledged universities; in time, two-year community colleges may seek to become four-year institutions. This is not necessarily in the state's best interests. It leads to the multiplication of similar programs, sometimes to the omission of programs that are needed, to inefficiency and waste. System trustees have the responsibility for distributing programs among state institutions in a sensible and equitable way.

3. **To safeguard institutional interests and needs.** Where institutional boards are absent, system boards have a special and delicate responsibility. Appointed or elected to serve the state as a whole, they are expected to be neutral in judging the claims of the system's members. Yet the individual institutions need protectors and advocates. No two are quite alike. Each deserves special consideration of some sort. In theory the officers of the system should be sensitive to the many subtle differences and needs of Upstate U and Downstate U, and many of them are. But not all, for the very size of the operation encourages the managers to impose uniform regulations. Trustees, standing apart from daily operations, can insist on special consideration.

4. **To maintain flexibility within the system.** This is closely related to the last item. Bureau-

cracies tend to grow rigid, especially when dealing with large numbers. Formulas take the place of individual decisions. In many cases they must, but not in all. They are always easier and tend therefore to dominate the decision making. It is hard for the officers who are trying to cope with a multitude of situations or instances not to fall back on formula thinking. It is the business of system trustees to discourage this and to insist that decision making within the system remain flexible.

5. **To prepare and defend long range state plans.** This is a natural corollary to the first responsibility above. To give thought to the educational needs of the state's citizens, however, is one thing; to construct long range plans for achieving educational goals is another. All that was said above about the importance of the trustees' role in demanding and approving long range plans for single institutions is *a fortiori* applicable to the trustees of statewide systems. In the best of times plans are an enormous asset. In the worst of times they are essential.

6. **To insulate institutions from political control.** When state universities were created, boards of trustees or regents were appointed (or elected) to take responsibility and oversight for the universities and to make certain that they were protected from direct political interference. The enormous concentration of people and money on postsecondary education since World War II has, to repeat what has already been pointed out, engendered a new public stake in our colleges and universities and a new demand that they be directly responsive to the public will. The creation of statewide governing and coordinating boards was a partial response to this demand.

What we are now witnessing is the attempt of legislatures, and even more of governors and their executive departments, to dictate through the statewide systems how the state's money shall be spent and how the institutions shall be run. Instead of appropriations to be spent at the discretion of the system and its members, appropriations come with line item instructions from the legislature's educational committee. In New York state, faculty salaries are negotiated with the union, not at the institutional level and not even at the statewide board level, but in the executive offices in Albany. System trustees should support, as we have seen, institutional autonomy to the extent possible by urging that decisions be decentralized. Their responsibility is also to safeguard the autonomy of the system by holding political pressure at arm's length. The great state universities cannot be run as regulated industries or like the state highway departments.

THE EFFECTIVE BOARD

Of all the issues that have been studied about higher education, the activities of boards of trustees is probably the least understood — and one of the most important.

(Baldridge, 1978)

Some governing boards are superb; some, alas, are the reverse; and the vast majority fall somewhere in between. Every board is capable of improvement, and in the past few years many have made real progress.

The last chapter focused on the responsibilities which trustees assume when they become members of a board. The effectiveness of a board, however, is more than the sum of the contributions of its individual members. The board is an organism, and the quality of its performance depends on a variety of organizational factors quite distinct from the individual abilities of the members who compose it. This chapter will explore the most important of those factors.

1. Joint Commitment

To accept membership on the board of a college or university is to make a tacit commitment to the institution—in Sproull's words, to make it worthy of survival and to make sure that it does. This is an individual commitment which can only be realized through the board's joint actions. An effective board must first of all be a committed board. The manifestation of individual enthusiasm and high responsibility becomes infectious; it can raise an indifferent board to a new level of responsibility and performance.

Commitment means work and the investment of time. One simple and highly visible test of trustee involvement is their attendance at board and committee meetings. In the 1967 Hartnett and Rauh survey of 5,000 trustees in 536 institutions, 53 percent reported that they had attended all board meetings (in the 1967 calendar year), 28 percent three-fourths or more of the meetings, 12 percent between one-half and three-quarters, and 3 percent fewer than one-half.[1] It can be argued that, since trustees are busy people, this is a remarkably good record. Yet the empty chair at the board table is always a bit depressing and can easily be contagious. On the contrary, full attendance gives a lift to the meeting and draws members back on a regular basis.

Public institutions generally schedule more board meetings per year (6-15) than private colleges and universities (mostly 3-4). This makes comparisons difficult. Since, however, the Hartnett/Rauh survey indicates no significant difference in attendance between the trustees of public and private institutions, public trustees would seem to work harder at their jobs.

A second measurement of trustee involvement is the total amount of time which trustees give to the job. Hartnett and Rauh asked their roster of trustees to list the number of hours per annum they spent on every form of trustee activity— board meetings, committee meetings, meetings with college groups, speeches, fund raising, conferences with college personnel, and other. The average came to 63.17 hours or 5.25 hours per month. The regents of state universities spent most time, 9.6 hours per month; the trustees of Catholic institutions least, 4.7 hours.[2] The increase in community colleges since 1967 has undoubtedly improved these figures.

It can be argued that a trustee's contribution should not be measured in purely quantitative terms. "Sometimes it is the quality of their insights," writes Rauh (1969), "the quickness of their minds, or the brilliance of their personalities which has an almost catalytic effect on the rest of

1. The report does not account for the missing 4 percent (Hartnett, 1969, p. 67).

2. Glenn Williams, vice president for student affairs at Eastern Illinois University, provides one additional bit of evidence. In a 1977 survey of 48 new members of statewide boards he found a range from four hours per month to 15 days each month. Two members testified that board service took one-third of their time. Two to four days was the pattern for most of the group (AGB Reports, November/December 1977).

the board" (p.110). He goes on to say, however, that a board cannot tolerate very many such individuals. Another defense of short-changing the institution is that money is more valuable than time, and no doubt there are college and university presidents who would willingly exchange board attendance and other activities for gifts of seven figures. If so inclined, it would be well to heed the words of Atherton Bean, businessman, philanthropist and member of the board of Carleton College:

> *It is popularly supposed that the only skill that a trustee needs is either the ability to give money (if that is a skill) or to persuade others to do so (which certainly is).... There is no particular reason why the possession of a few million dollars and recurrent generous impulses should act to keep a person off a college board. However, the fact of the matter is that, at least in my experience, very few trustees have been chosen for that narrow combination of "virtues." I can visualize choosing a very limited number of trustees for wealth alone, but in my book the person who is willing to contribute no more than money is of marginal worth* (AGB Reports, May/June 1975).

2. Board Composition

The standard criticism of governing boards has been the elleged monolithic character of their has been the alleged monolithic character of their membership—white, Anglo-Saxon, Protestant, male, well-to-do business and professional men, over 50 in age—in short, the "establishment" with all its basic conservatism. The most recent survey of college and university trustees was made in 1976 at the request of AGB by Irene Gomberg and Frank Atelsek of the American Council on Education. In summary, 85 percent of all trustees were then male, 15 percent female, with single campus public boards having the highest percentage of women (18 percent). In terms of race 93 percent were white, 6 percent black, and 1 percent other minorities, with public single campus boards again in the lead with 14 percent minorities. These figures are slowly improving. In age, 66 percent were over 50; 9.5 percent under 40. Ninety percent had baccalaureate degrees, and of these 32 percent had advanced doctoral or professional degrees.[3]

There are over 700 church-related or religiously affiliated colleges and universities in this country. A hundred years ago one would have found members (usually clergy) of the sponsoring religious organizations on each of their boards, more often than not selected or appointed by the sponsoring church or religious order. In this century, religious control has lessened. Among Protestant colleges there is growing conviction that boards should determine their own membership.

Largely as a result of the liberal thrust of the Twenty-First Ecumenical Council in Rome, 1963-65, Catholic colleges and universities have been rapidly divesting themselves of clerical control. In a survey of 134 Catholic institutions, Martin J. Stamm found that 60 percent now have independent governing boards and 93 percent have lay as well as clerical board members, and the actual number of lay trustees constituted 62 percent of all trustees of the Catholic colleges and universities included in the study.[4]

3. The Gomberg/Atelsek survey was published in 1977 by the American Council on Education as Higher Education Panel Report, Number 35, with the title Composition of College and University Governing Boards. A summary of the survey is to be found in "Who's on the Governing Board?" by the authors in AGB Reports, Nov./Dec. 1977. Since there is so much interest in the biographical character of trustees, the tables giving complete information are reprinted in appendix A. Other recent studies are the Hartnett/Ruml survey of 1968 and the Research Triangle Institute survey published in 1974. The figures do not vary significantly, and such variations as do appear are rendered suspect due to the different samples used. The most recent and probably the best inventory of trustee characteristics is to be found in Gomberg/Atelsek.

4. See the articles by Richard T. Ingram on church-related colleges and by Martin J. Stamm on Catholic institutions in Current Issues in Catholic Higher Education, Vol. 2, No. 1 (Summer 1981).

5. See Peter K. Mills, "Community College Trustees: A Survey" in the AGB publication The Two-Year College Trustee, 1972. Also Sandra I. Drake, Research Report: A Study of Community and Junior College Boards of Trustees published by the American Association of Community and Junior Colleges, 1977.

Surveys of community and junior college trustees indicate that in public institutions, 85 percent are male and 15 percent female, whereas in independent two-year institutions the ratio is 77 percent to 23 percent. In the public college 91 percent of trustees are white, 6 percent black, and 3 percent other minorities; in the independent college the figures are 92, 5 and 3 percent. Fifty-five percent of the public trustees and 63 percent of the independent are 50 years of age or older; 13 percent and 11 percent are under 40. Businessmen constitute one-third of the trustees in both sectors; professional people (excluding education) make up 19 percent of the private boards, 14 percent of the public.[5]

The 1976 census of the trustee population indicates that governing boards have indeed been skewed in favor of males, whites and age. This has been the cultural power pattern of the American, and indeed Western, society. Is it the best pattern for the governance of higher education in this country? Partly because it fits in with the temper of the times, partly based on sounder reasoning, an increasing number of students of academic governance answer the question in the negative. A truly effective board is more likely to be composed of individuals who bring diverse experiences, talents, and attitudes to the resolution of institutional problems.

Colleges and universities need trustees with different professional skills to advise administrative officers where to turn for sound advice. They need trustees with different experiences and different backgrounds to hammer out a sensible meeting of minds. The more complex the institution, the more important it becomes to distill a collective decision from the views of people familiar with different phases of its many operations and understanding of its different constituencies.

The advocates of faculty and student membership on governing boards make use of this argument. Faculty have insisted for a long time that they know more about teaching and learning than do the trustees, and they are right. Some faculty then argue that they should sit on the board and point to the British pattern of faculty control. Apart from the *non sequitur*, the claim ignores the inherent and inescapable conflict of interest which would result. Trustees must decide what is in the best interest of the institution as a whole, and faculty prerogatives (rank, salary, leaves, teaching loads, research, and the like), however central to the processes and programs of education, are still a part only of total operations. The problem is not merely conflict between faculty interests and the broader interests of the institution. There are many conflicts of interest inside the faculty, and to have these carried by faculty members into boards of trustees would be unhealthy and dangerous. The spread of collective bargaining with its obviously adversarial character is the most dramatic indication of the conflict of interest.

Student demands for representation on boards erupted in the '60s and have continued at a less shrill level since then. Quite a number of colleges and universities have appointed or elected students to their boards, some with voting power and some without, more in the public than in the private sector. The results so far have been inconclusive. No serious troubles have been reported, and some boards have found the student contribution quite helpful. Certainly, students as well as faculty points of view are important, and boards should make special efforts to receive and to understand them.

But does this require that students serve on boards? There are other and better ways of getting at student opinion. The same problem of conflict of interest arises with students as with faculty, though the nature of the conflict is different. Furthermore, very few students—let us be honest about it—are ready for the responsibilities of trusteeship. They see problems in terms of their personal needs and plans. They serve too short a time to master all they need to know, nor will they be around to live with the consequences of their decisions. It is important for the health of higher education that there be substantial contributions from faculty and from students to the decisions made by governing boards. They are where the action is and they know what it is like. But their contributions will be more effective if made to the board rather than on the board.[6]

Every board could profit from having at least one educator as a member. A faculty member from another institution (preferably a non-competitive one) is in a position to interpret faculty problems and attitudes which the board as a whole will need to understand. Another administrative officer can reinforce (or correct if necessary) the president's recommendations stemming from trends or changes affecting higher education across the country. And some boards are finding it very helpful to elect young graduates just out of college who can contribute something close to a student point of view but with a certain perspective, and who assume the same responsibilities

6. This is the conclusion to which the Carnegie Commission on Higher Education came. See Chapter 5 of the Governance of Higher Education. It is also the conclusion of the National Commission on Trustee Selection which issued reports in 1980 for improving the selection of trustees in both public and private institutions (published by AGB). Harold W. Dodds, former president of Princeton, has some trenchant comments on the subject of professors as board members in The Academic President— Educator or Caretaker? (McGraw-Hill Book Co. 1962, pp. 225-30).

as all board members of the institution.

3. Selection of Trustees

"The most important job of the board," writes John Knudsen, vice president of St. Edward's University in Texas, "is not hiring and firing the president, but selecting the trustees. Weak trustees will spend much time picking weak presidents. Pick good trustees, build solid committees, monitor the board operations, and the rest falls into place—even great presidents" (Frantzreb, Ed., 1981, p.40). While this comment departs from the generally accepted view, it does call attention to the very great importance of creating a strong board. The publication within the last two years of excellent analyses and recommendations for improving the recruitment of trustees makes it unnecessary to do more than emphasize the major considerations in this section.[7]

One starts with some thought about the nature of the institution—its problems, prospects, and needs. A locally oriented college will have different requirements from those of a national university, a private from a public institution. What talents does the institution need on its board? The next step is to examine the qualifications of the present members of the board—their strengths, weaknesses, special skills. Gale offers a useful checklist in his chapter in the Ingram *Handbook*. Francis Pray proposes a series of questions: Is a high degree of financial competence represented on the board? Legal competence? Experience in higher education? Top management and business competence? And so on.[8]

A third step, which might in fact precede the first two and carry them out, is the appointment

7. See Association of Governing Boards (1980a) and (1980b); and Gale. "Selecting and Deploying Trustees" in Ingram (Ed.) 1980.

8. "Trusteemanship for Colleges and Universities," published by the Council for Financial Aid to Education (undated).

60

of a nominating or membership or trustee committee to engage in a continuous process of collecting the names of potential trustees, of investigating their special talents or contributions, and of recommending candidates appropriate to the places to be filled. Such a committee would presumably request and welcome suggestions from all sources. It would regularly assess the quality of the board, both in terms of skills and of diversity of background, age, sex, race, location, religion (if relevant), and political affiliation (again if relevant). Obviously in public institutions such committees, if they exist at all, will be purely advisory to the appointing authority.

Two issues continue to plague the business of building proper college and university boards. The first is the problem of legitimacy in the broadest sense of that term. It might better be called the question of moral authority. How does a board gain respect so that its decisions are accepted without protest? Calkins in the article already quoted (1975) suggests that "The majority of the board should be selected by some process which is demonstrably difficult to manipulate" (p.25). He cites the Harvard Board of Overseers, all elected by alumni vote, as an example.

The method of election or selection or appointment is certainly one factor, but the competence and performance of any governing body are even more important. A public board composed of outstanding and public-spirited citizens commands respect. So does a private board whose membership exhibits a genuine concern for different points of view.

The second issue concerns representation. The responsibility of a trustee is to seek the best interests of the institution as a whole and not to be the advocate of some constituency. The trustee of the private as well as the public institution holds a public trust. This is quite consistent with a deliberately sought diversity. Trustees cannot and should not avoid seeing problems in the first instance in terms of their own backgrounds; they can and should reach decisions in terms of a common good.

The boards of almost all private colleges and universities are self-perpetuating. This freedom has led to haphazard and careless procedures in many instances; it also provides the ideal opportunity for building strong and effective boards. Most private institutions have found it desirable to let their alumni fill a designated number of places, not because alumni should be "represented" as such, but because they constitute a natural group of individuals committed to their colleges. The appointment or election of a certain number of trustees by the sponsoring religious body of a church-related college or university presents a more difficult problem. The desire to maintain denominational influence or control is understandable, but it puts the final composition of the governing board outside board control. The appointing agency or group is not necessarily privy to the needs of the board or sensitive to the requirements of trusteeship. Consultations between the board and the appointing agency can be helpful.

In four-year public institutions, 75 percent of the trustees or regents are appointed by the governor or some other state official, usually with the consent of at least one house of the legislature. In five states regents are chosen by public election.

Public elections in which candidates run for office on party lines (which are irrelevant to university problems), or on a reform-the-university platform (which is inconsistent with the impartial role of the trustee), would seem to be the least satisfactory way of choosing trustees[9] By their very nature they embroil the university in partisan politics. Gubernatorial appointment with legislative confirmation is preferable, but even here too many appointments are made on political rather than qualitative grounds.

Lee and Bowen, students of state university systems, take a dim view of the situation. "The selection system falls short on at least three counts. The boards are highly unrepresentative of the society served by the university. They do not possess legitimacy in the minds of those most directly affected by their power. They are not sufficiently independent of partisan political currents…In the context of the 1970s, a governor can no more ignore political considerations in the selection of trustees and in their subsequent activities than deny the reality of the next election" (*AGB Reports*, March 1972, pp.21-2). Lee and Bowen, and more recently the National Commission on College and University Trustee Selection, recommend the establishment of blue ribbon or special committees to nominate candidates from among whom the governor will make his or her choice as the most effective way of reducing the political aspect and enhancing the qualitative aspect of public trustee appointments.

Independent junior colleges enjoy the same opportunities and face the same problems in the choice of the members of their boards as we saw above with respect to four-year private institu-

9. Robben W. Fleming, former president of the University of Michigan, disagrees with this conclusion. See his comments in AGB Reports, Nov./Dec. 1975.

tions. In the case of the public community colleges, between 50 percent and 60 percent of their trustees are elected locally. The others are appointed by the governor or by a local authority or by the two together. Party politics plays a much smaller part in local elections, but where the governor appoints they can be as pernicious as with four-year institutions.

Public elections do not necessarily provide the kind of trustees the community college may need, but in a 1977 survey, 60 percent of chairmen and presidents ranked their boards as very effective (Drake, 1977). In an earlier survey it was found that a majority of trustees would prefer some broadening of membership and favored the governance model of the four-year state colleges rather than that of the local school boards (Mills, 1972). A local screening or nominating committee composed of prominent local citizens could do much to improve the quality of gubernatorial appointments, and its endorsement might influence the results of public election.

4. Trustee Orientation

One of the responsibilities of trustees discussed in the preceding chapter was the responsibility to be well informed. That means that trustees must be educated. The individual serving as trustee for the very first time needs education on the nature of trusteeship. Those serving for the first time on a particular board need orientation on the history, organization and peculiarities of the college or university. All trustees, old as well as new, need exposure from time to time on the issues and problems of higher education particularly as they affect their institution.

In a national survey in 1974 of four-year and two-year, public and private, institutions (Nelson and Turk, 1974) one-third reported that some kind of systematic orientation for new members was provided. In recent years much attention has been drawn to the importance of educating trustees, and a variety of educational experiments have been tried. If the time and effort recommended in the preceding section are devoted to the proper selection of trustees, there is no excuse for failing to provide an orientation program. It will pay a substantial dividend.

There are at least three phases and kinds of indoctrination. The first should take place at or around the time the invitation to the board is offered or accepted. Presumably the president and the chairman of the board (or some other combination) will see the prospective trustee in person. They should make clear that they are asking the individual to take on an important and demanding assignment, that it will involve time including attendance at board and committee meetings, that it will mean participation in a variety of significant educational decisions, and that (if a private college or university) all trustees are expected to share in giving and asking for money. They should sketch briefly the status of the institution, its strong and weak points, its problems and prospects in the near future. If the individual being asked to serve has had no prior experience as a college or university trustee, the president and the chairman would do well to suggest (the president might promise to send) one or two books or pamphlets on trusteeship.[10]

The second stage comes after the new trustee has joined the board, normally around the time

10. The Handbook of College and University Trusteeship (Ingram, 1980) is by all odds the best and most complete coverage of the subject. J.L. Zwingle's Effective Trusteeship, published by AGB, is an excellent short treatment by an expert. Myron F. Wicke has a short Handbook for Trustees focused on church-related colleges, published by the Board of Education of the Methodist Church. The Association of Community College Trustees issued in 1977 a quite practical Handbook for Community College and Technical Institute Trustees under the title Trusteeship, written by George E. Potter. It may, however, prove too much for most new trustees, since it is designed as a permanent resource rather than an introduction.

of his or her first board meeting. At this point it is important for the new trustee to get acquainted with the college or university. This can be done in any number of ways, including a full day on campus for a tour of inspection, meeting and talking with the chief administrative officers, exploring those areas in which the trustee is particularly interested, possibly sitting in on a class or attending a public lecture or other event. Some institutions have manuals prepared for each trustee consisting of bylaws of the board, faculty and student organizations, presidential reports, minutes of recent board meetings, and the like. Other institutions schedule formal meetings with the new trustees with programs which might include brief reports from the deans of various schools and other officers. Another variation is the "trustee-in-residence," a device which enables the new trustee to get the feel of the campus through exposure to students, faculty and administration usually over a period of two days to a week.

The third phase in the education of trustees, and a very important one it is, consists of *special* board meetings to explore and discuss the major problems and impending issues which are of current concern to higher education and which will affect the policies and operations of the college or university. Ideally these special meetings should be workshops or retreats which fall outside the regular schedule of meetings, but they can also be one of the regular meetings designated for the special purpose of discussing major concerns or even a major concern. The normal board meeting tends to get cluttered up with routine matters which absorb time and energy and prevent trustees from considering the truly significant issues which need their best judgment. Does the board or the college need reorganization? Does the new long-range plan makes sense? These are just a sample of the many issues which an effective board should be considering.[11]

5. Continuity and Change

At the beginning of the last chapter it was noted that we count on governing boards to provide a certain continuity and stability to colleges and universities. Trustees, as we saw, have a special obligation to safeguard the integrity of the institution. They are the ones who look to the past to make sure that present operations are consistent with the original purposes as set forth in charter or statute or as modified by action of previous boards. They have responsibility for the preservation of the trust and must, therefore, see to it that present practices do not jeopardize future operations.

Good trustees are therefore to be cherished, but all good things sooner or later come to an end. In time trustees like other mortals run out of new ideas. They cling to old familiar ways. Their attitudes become fixed. They grow fearful of change.

All, that is, but the very exceptional. For public institutions this is generally not a problem since most trustees are appointed for fixed terms and reappointment is the exception. It is interesting to note in the Research Triangle Institute survey that 11 percent of the responding trustees had served for 20 years or more (Davis and Batchelor, 1974). In the same survey, 60 percent of the presidents indicated that the replacement of one or more board members would improve the functioning of the board. This was the highest response

11. Richard T. Ingram's excellent chapter, "Assuring Trustee Orientation and Development," in the Handbook (Ingram, 1980) explores these and related ideas with a wealth of suggestive detail.

to a series of options on factors that might improve governing boards.

A vital and effective board needs (1) a mandatory retirement provision and (2) some limitation on the number of consecutive years or terms a board member may serve. It needs the first to safeguard itself against intellectual dry rot. To be sure, some men and women in their eighties are more alive, more forward looking, more contemporary in their sympathies than others in their thirties. The loss of their presence is the price paid for the avoidance of an over-age board, out of touch with the contemporary world. A board needs the second rule to insure a constantly fresh flow of ideas and points of view. A board must constantly be trying to recreate itself.

Lengths of terms and age limitations are generally set by law for trustees of public institutions. Some will argue that boards of private institutions can achieve all this by wise management and without arbitrary rules. More power to them. If nominating committees, as suggested in section 3, will consistently assess the quality of the current membership before recommending renewed appointments, dead wood can be eliminated. But it involves an honest tough-minded appraisal followed by firm action in parting company. Most boards are reluctant to hurt someone's feelings, especially if it risks alienating an actual or potential donor.

A mandatory rotation system which limits by statute the number of successive years or terms a trustee may serve is in many ways the easiest and most graceful way of resolving the problem. The National Commission on Trustee Selection (AGB, 1980) strongly recommends that trustees be limited to 12 consecutive years, with not more than two, six-year terms for public trustees and three terms of three or four years for private trustees. On the private side it is always possible to re-elect a very valuable trustee after a year's sabbatical; indeed, his or her interest can be maintained by continued voluntary service on one or more board committees. Election to honorary or emeritus status with the right to attend and to participate in meetings, but not to vote, is another way of recognizing the contribution of an outstanding trustee.

6. Board Size

Governing boards range in size from five to 80. Among public institutions, both two-year and four-year, the great majority have seven to 10 members, the actual number normally being set by statute. Private institutions have larger boards, the majority falling between 20 and 40. The average for independent colleges and universities is 24, for church-related colleges excluding the Roman Catholic 27, and for Catholic colleges and universities, 20.[12]

The chief criticisms of large boards are three. First, it is alleged that only quite small groups can truly deliberate on the complex issues facing boards and that, therefore, large boards tend toward *pro forma* approval of administrative recommendations. Second, members of large boards tend to lose interest because they do not feel personally involved. They let others take responsibility for assignments or decisions. Their attendance at meetings becomes irregular. Third, since it is more difficult to bring large than small boards together, some inner group, usually the

12. *The figure for Roman Catholic institutions shows a marked increase in the last 20 years due largely to the addition of lay members. In 1960 the average number was just under eight.*

executive committee, takes over on behalf of the board. If the executive committee is clearly subordinate to the board, acting in its absence and submitting its decisions to the full board for confirmation or the reverse, this arrangement can work very well. If, however, the executive committee or inner group supplants the board, the other members may feel relegated to second-class status and will cease to be interested and active trustees.

The ctitics of small boards, on the other hand, point out that they fail to reflect a sufficient variety of points of view, that they are correspondingly less able to deal wisely with issues confronting the institution, and that it is easy for them to become a too closely knit group or to be paralyzed by factionalism. It has also been argued, and there is some evidence in support of this criticism, that small boards are more inclined to get involved in administrative decisions rather than being limited to policy matters.[13]

There is in short no simple or obvious answer to the question about the proper size of boards. Public institutions are less flexible in size since board positions are mandated by state law. This may have influenced the responses of both trustees and presidents to the question whether an increase or decrease in size would improve board functioning. In none of the three categories of institution (two-year, four-year state college, state university) did the percentage favoring change in size reach as high as 15 percent, and such few as did recommend change favored an increase rather than a decrease. Among private institutions with their greater freedom to change, the responses showed some disposition, especially on the part of

13. See Houle: The Effective Board, pp.58-61, for a useful discussion of the pros and cons of size.

70

trustees, to favor smaller boards (22 percent of university trustees and 19 percent of college trustees), but none of these figures shows any widespread dissatisfaction with board size.[14]

Size should be determined chiefly by function. Private colleges and universities depend heavily on raising money from private sources. This need virtually dictates a large board composed both of generous donors and of individuals prepared to participate in fund raising efforts. The optimum size will also be influenced by such factors as the frequency of meetings, the board structure, and the amount of time board members are prepared to contribute. The decision is a pragmatic one. But clearly, the effective size is whatever best serves the major requirements of the board of that institution.

7. Committee Structure

Among American organizations of almost every kind the standard procedure is to appoint committees to perform specific tasks or to take responsibility for specific areas of activity. This divides up the work. It makes use of special skills. It provides a form of involvement. It is generally considered an orderly and efficient form of group action.[15] And so we find that most governing boards establish standing committees to supervise various aspects of the institution's operations and appoint from time to time *ad hoc* committees for special purposes (such as the selection of a new president). Many community colleges (60 percent) and a substantial number of state colleges and universities do not employ the committee system. With their small numbers and frequent meetings they prefer to function as committees of the whole.

14. Davis and Batchelor, 1974, pp. 43-45.

15. But a cautionary note is supplied by the old saw according to which a committee consists of the incompetent, appointed by the unwilling, to do the unnecessary.

That committees generally serve a useful purpose is testified to by their extensive use and by the evidence of the Research Triangle Institute survey. Recipients were asked to what extent each of 10 factors operated in the process of making decisions by their boards. Over half the trustees checked "strong guidance by committees or committee chairmen." Only "recommendations by the president" ranked higher as an influencing factor.

The illustrative bylaws developed by the Association of Governing Boards (Ingram, 1980, Resource C) lists 10 committees: executive, nominating, educational affairs, faculty affairs, student affairs, finance, audit, development, investment, and buildings and grounds. Modern multiversities may need more; small colleges can manage well with fewer. In an interesting essay entitled "The State of the Art of College Trusteeship," Francis Pray (1974) suggests that there are certain dangers in the multiplication of committees (narrowness of oversight, duplication of effort, failure to see the whole picture) and that a better strategy would be to have five major committees—executive, nominating (he calls it committee on trustees), planning and budget, educational affairs, and resource management. Other committees would be subsumed under the last three mentioned.

A quite different suggestion is made by Rauh (1969, pp.82-3). "The proposal I would make," he writes, "is that standing committees be replaced by ad hoc committees convened to perform specific tasks." In support of this position he argues that trustee time would be more functionally and constructively used, that the committee's membership could be better suited to the problem, that

72

the identification of the special task would tend to direct attention to the broader issues, that trustees would have a clearer feeling of involvement, and that it might be more practical in that a busy trustee reluctant to commit himself or herself to a continuing committee assignment might be able to free up a block of time for a limited one. This approach may be too radical a departure for most boards, but it does call attention to the need for giving careful thought to the structuring of the board.

One or two further cautions are in order. Committees should have clear assignments which are both necessary and constructive. They should meet either at regularly scheduled times or frequently enough to have significant reports for the board as a whole. Those reports should in most cases be presented in writing in advance, so that board members will have time to digest the contents and be prepared to ask questions. The scheduling of committee meetings the afternoon or evening before board meetings, while sometimes unavoidable when membership is widely scattered and expensive to bring together, should be avoided as much as possible. It not only tends to rush committee discussion, but also renders impossible presentation of committee reports in time for advance consideration. Every committee should have a college officer to serve as staff and liaison in order to facilitate the work and deliberations of the committee.

Some rotation of committee membership is desirable not only to provide experience and involvement for board members, but also to prevent an entrenched bloc within the board. Committees that continue with the same membership for a long period of time can become very powerful and usurp certain of the decision making functions of the board as a whole. This is a particular danger when the chairman remains so long in office that no one dares say him or her nay (Wood, 1982).

The danger that the executive committee may usurp the function of the board as a whole was discussed briefly in the preceding section. This consequence is by no means inevitable. Sensitivity on the part of members of the executive committee, awareness of the potential danger on the part of the chairman of the board and the president, rotation of membership, scrupulous insistence that the minutes of the executive committee be provided for all trustees and that all actions of the committee be reviewed and approved by the board as a whole, will avoid the danger of an inner cabinet. It takes thought, however. The most effective structure does not happen by itself.

8. Frequency and Length of Meetings

Frequency of board meetings is in inverse ratio to size. Community and state colleges and universities, with their relatively small boards, meet most frequently. Fifty percent of community college boards meet nine or more times per year, as do 36 percent of state college boards and 63 percent of state university boards. On the other hand, 60 percent of independent college and university boards meet only three to four times per year. Seven percent of private college boards and 12 percent of private university boards meet as often as nine times per year. Seventy-nine percent of black college boards meet only once or

74

16. Data taken from Hartnett and
    Rauh, 1969; Davis and Batchelor,
    1974; Drake, 1977.

twice a year.[16] Large boards, and particularly those with national as distinct from local membership, find it inconvenient to meet very frequently.

There tends also to be an inverse ratio between frequency and length of meeting. The once or twice a month meetings of community college boards are normally limited to an afternoon or evening. There is rarely time for extended discussion of long-range issues, attention being focused on practical problems needing quick decisions. This leads, as was noted earlier, to a tendency on the part of community college trustees to get involved with the business of administration. The less frequent meetings of private institutional boards are likely to extend over one or two days. This allows time for much greater discussion of important issues, for more attention to be given to where the institution stands and where it is headed. This is an advantage which we shall explore further in the section on board agenda.

It should be noted that the boards of many state universities, whether governing a single institution or a system, meet for one or two full days each month. This gives them the advantage of both frequency and depth. On balance the trustees and regents of state institutions work harder at their job than do the trustees of private colleges and universities. At least the data on time contributed to service as a trustee support this conclusion.

9. Agenda for Board Meetings

"Not all board meetings are dull; some of them are cancelled," according to one disgruntled trustee cited by Houle (1960, p.131). There is no excuse for this state of affairs.

There are at least three wrong patterns of board meetings, all of which are far too common. The first is to overload the agenda with minutiae until there is no time for discussion and decisions on important issues.[17] Such routine items, as they are usually called, should be kept off the agenda or swept through in a hurry, preferably at the end of the meeting. Board approval of all faculty appointments, promotions and salaries, mandated in many public institutions by statute and in private ones by bylaws, is an anachronism and a waste of valuable board time.

A second mistake is to fill the time available for board meetings with lengthy formal reports. It is customary to have reports from various standing committees. Some chairmen drone on at unconscionable length, telling the board more about penguins than they care to know about penguins. Written reports circulated in advance of the meeting, as suggested in Section 7, would make long oral reports unnecessary and allow the board to concentrate on whatever controversial or decisive actions were needed. When committee reports are followed, or preceded, by reports from vice presidents, provosts and sometimes deans and then capped by a "state of the college" report (a "stand up speech" as one trustee described it) by the president, there is apt to be little time for participation by the trustees. Their time is wasted and their contribution lost.

A third pattern leading often to uncomfortable and unprofitable results is one in which the president dumps before the assembled board for immediate decision one or more urgent issues of some importance to the institution. The consequences of a postponed decision can be costly

17. Consider the appalling picture presented by Paltridge, Hurst and Morgan (1973) in their study of the actions, as recorded in the minutes of 19 state university boards for a period of one year. This is summarized by Paltridge in AGB Reports, March 1974, where he comments: "The most significant finding is that boards undertake a tremendous volume of decision actions in the course of a year's meetings, and that much of this volume consists of pro forma actions on long lists of detailed operational matters. The responsibility for policy formulation, long-term planning, administrative guidance, review of performance, and support of the institution in the realization of its goals are frequently given minor attention or left to the initiative of administrators or governmental agencies" (p. 21).

or inconvenient. There is not adequate time for thoughtful consideration, no background material having been provided. The president presents a strong recommendation. Failure to support the recommendation may be interpreted as undermining the president's position and authority. So the vote to approve is passed, and the trustees return home uncomfortable, dissatisfied, and apprehensive at having acted in haste and with inadequate information.

The purpose of a board meeting is to reach agreement (as close to consensus as possible) on important issues on the basis of adequate information and intelligent discussion. Charles Nelson suggests four steps to achieve this purpose (AGB Reports, Sept./Oct. 1979).

1. Put the important policy issues at the beginning of the meeting when the trustees are fresh, not at the end when they may be tired and anxious to get away.

2. At least once a year, include on the agenda for discussion an impending major problem or development. The purpose would be to alert the board well in advance to an issue which will at some future date require their best judgment. An immediate decision is not required, indeed not wanted. This is an educational exercise. Some decisions need marinating. A forewarned board with time to reflect will arrive at wiser decisions.

3. When issues come up for decision, present the alternatives. Should the university join with commercial interests in genetic research? What policies will the college or university follow in the face of current trends toward more professionalized sports programs? These are complex issues presenting multiple options. Board discussion

should not be focused only on the recommendation by the president. It should be based on a consideration of the several possible policies open to the institution. These should be clearly presented. Proponents of different solutions might be invited to present their arguments.

4. Make sure that every item on the agenda has been subjected to "a harsh test of relevance." Is it necessary but of no great significance? Get it over with quickly. Is it important? Allow plenty of time for it. Is it neither? Cross it off.

What this comes down to is that the agenda must be planned in advance with the most careful thought to the best use of the collective time and wisdom of the board. It should be done through consultation between the president and the chairman. Board members should feel free to suggest topics for consideration. Rauh even raises the interesting question of what might result from inviting faculty and students to propose the three subjects they would like most to have the board discuss (1969, p.84). Background material should be prepared, as suggested above. It will take not a little skill to provide all the relevant information in concise enough form for the busy trustee. Arrangements for the appearance of resource people if needed should be made.

The president and the chairman might well ask themselves, what is it we want this board meeting to accomplish? Clearly certain decisions need to be reached. This may involve discussing the problem with key board members in advance of the meeting. It may involve a calculus of which board members have or are likely to have one view and which another, and how they are to be brought into agreement. Also one would like to have all members of the board participate actively in the discussion and decision. And one hopes that as the trustees return home they will have a sense of excitement, of satisfaction and of accomplishment returning with them.

The place of the meeting and its atmosphere or tone can be positive or negative influences. It is preferable—though sometimes not convenient—to hold meetings at the institution where trustees can feel physically involved in the "trust" for which they are responsible. The size, shape and decor of the meeting room is also important. Lighting and seating arrangements can make trustees uncomfortable or relaxed. Are the necessary documents, paper and pencils, at each trustee's place? Do meetings begin on time? Are there breaks for coffee or other refreshments? The degree of formality or informality with which the meeting is conducted will depend on the temperament of the chairman. There should be enough formality to follow an agenda and to allow motions to be made and acted on. Too formal a meeting, however, inhibits discussion. Trustees should feel geared up for action, yet relaxed enough to feel comfortable with one another, to disagree without embarrassment, and to change their minds when the arguments are convincing.

10. Open Versus Closed Meetings

Most, if not all, governing boards would find the relaxed and free atmosphere described in the preceding section more easily realized in private than in public meetings. The advantages of privacy for the discussion of delicate or controversial issues are very great, and the trustees of private colleges and universities have been loath to give

them up. According to an Indiana University survey of 1968, only 25 percent of private boards permitted individuals not directly involved with board business to sit in on their meetings. The figure may be higher now. It would be reasonable to assume that the individuals not directly involved with board business would be members of the academic community.

According to the same Indiana University study, 89 percent of the board meetings of public institutions are open to the public. Sunshine laws have been adopted in many states putting severe limitations on the freedom of regents or trustees to discuss any institutional business in private. The majority of these laws, however, do provide for executive session to deal with highly confidential matters such as grounds for faculty or staff dismissals, comparison of the qualifications of candidates for the presidency, business negotiations where publicity might result in escalation of price, and the like. But it should be noted that in some states such as Florida, even meetings of the search and selection committee are open to the press and public, and all letters of reference regarding candidates are available for public inspection.

The public has a right to know; so runs the basic argument. But does it really? Or more accurately, what does it have a right to know? In the tax-supported public institution it has the right to know the decisions and the arguments supporting those decisions. James Dunseath, former president of the Arizona Board of Regents, insists, however, that: "A jury's deliberations are not public any more than are the editorial conferences of newspapers. It is no more appropriate to re-

18. *From an address entitled "Open Meetings – A Threat to Effective Governance," delivered in 1970 to the faculty and students of the University of Arizona.*

quire a board of regents to bare its discussions than it is to require an editor or publisher to reveal the discussion which occurs while he determines editorial policy."[18]

One gets mixed reports on the way sunshine laws work. Some presidents report that they are inconvenient, but can be lived with. In a survey of community colleges (Drake, 1977), 74 percent of the chairmen and 87 percent of the presidents said that on the whole sunshine laws work very well. Others find them close to disaster. In one state participants on a search and selection committee for a new president reported that they lost approximately one-third of their candidates (and unfortunately the best third) because all names were made public, and that it took them one-third more time to reach a decision because all discussion of candidates was out in the open. Quite apart from such delicate matters the costs of open meetings are considerable. One speaks more cautiously in public meetings, expresses one's views (and prejudices) less candidly, changes one's mind less easily, becomes too concerned with projecting a public image.

We must recognize, however, that the old era of secrecy in academic councils is being challenged. The changes in college and university population, expectations and attitudes, discussed in an earlier chapter of this study, are destroying the old pattern. The democratic and egalitarian pressures on governance are part of the new outlook. Since governing boards have real influence over issues affecting students, faculty, townspeople, taxpayers, it becomes in the modern temper increasingly difficult to exclude these interested groups from the meetings where their interests are being decided. The larger public education looms in state operations, the greater will be the demand for complete exposure.

For private institutions the issue is not one of legal necessity but of practical expediency. In a sense it is one aspect of legitimacy. What is secret is suspect. When exposed to the complexity of a problem, people tend to have greater sympathy for those struggling to find a reasonable solution. Those private instituions which have recently experimented with open meetings have in general found the results less awkward than anticipated.[19] Perhaps the best solution is to mix open with closed meetings or to invite special groups, say of faculty or students, to be present when certain issues are discussed. Open meetings are a mixed bag. Some day the pendulum may swing back, but for the nonce we would do well to recognize the current fashion and be prepared to defend our positions largely naked to the world.

11. Role of the Chairman

By virtue of his or her position the chairman is, or ought to be, the most important trustee. Over and above all the standard responsibilities of trustees, he or she has the special responsibility of leadership. The chairman, as was noted, participates in shaping the agenda and is solely responsible for the conduct of board meetings. Quietly, but decisively when necessary, he or she must direct board discussion, head off digressions, assist in getting problems clearly and fairly presented, and know when the time has come for a decision. The chairman is expected not only to know more about the institution than other trustees but to have a better grasp of educational issues. In

19. See Rauh (1969, p.149) in support of this view.

82

Frantzreb's words (1974) "chairmen must possess strong intestinal fortitude. They must live with unpopular decisions, recalcitrant presidents, loquacious trustees, difficult problem people—politicians, faculty, parents, businessmen, associations, media personnel. Here is where fairness, respect, and understanding as personal attributes come into play."

Among private institutions the chairman along with the president has a special concern for moulding the members into an effective organization. Among public institutions where regents or trustees are appointed by the state or a local authority, the chairman can often be influential in getting the right appointment. In both the public and the private sectors the chairman must moderate as well as lead—a healer of breaches, harmoniser of divisiveness, sometimes cajoler and, when necessary, a disciplinarian.[20] To the public the chairman is the symbol of the board and very often its spokesman. Within the board the chairman sets the example for the other trustees by his or her personal performance.

How long should any one individual serve as chairman? Frantzreb (1974) argues that "no person should remain as chairman for more than five years." But when a board enjoys an outstanding chairman, this becomes an arbitrary deprivation. Some public institutions rotate the chairmanship every year. I suspect this does not allow for development of a proper relationship with the president. Every chairman should begin looking for his or her successor at once, and no chairman, no matter how good, should continue indefinitely in office, for the longer the term, the more traumatic the eventual change. In addition, with some chair-

20. "Conflicts within governing boards are almost inevitable. Controversy is in itself not altogether bad if it leads to clarification and ultimate settlement of policy; but quarrelsomeness and continued vendettas are a drain on the energies of board and staff alike, and a substantial cost to the institution" (Zwingle, 1981, p. 30).

men (not those who are a joy forever) there is a danger that a slightly proprietary attitude will develop if too long in office. The special position of authority, the inside knowledge, the intimate relation with the president have been known to produce this effect; and along with it sometimes goes a tendency to intervene in the administration itself. These are dangers to be guarded against, primarily by the good sense of the chairman and other trustees, but also through the precaution that the chairman does not remain in office too long. This is an argument for some set limit by which all must abide, and it avoids the embarrassment of easing out a reluctant and probably difficult chairman.

In some institutions of higher education the president serves as chairman. Former President Dodds of Princeton thought this the proper arrangement. "There are both psychological and symbolic values involved here which emphasize that education is the principal purpose for which the university and board exist" (Dodds, 1962). Former President Fleming of Michigan argued that as chairman and presiding officer of the University's board he was in a stronger position than otherwise (Fleming, 1975). Most presidents would take the opposite view. The president needs someone to whom he or she can turn for counsel and even comfort. Who will look after the president's well-being except the chairman? To whom do critics of the president go if not to the chairman? The president needs a chairman, just as the chairman needs the president.

Robert Greenleaf has argued that a truly responsible board needs a chairman who will give full time to the job (Greenleaf, 1974). Although this seems to work at the Massachusetts Institute of Technology, it has not lasted long at other institutions. One ends up with two full-time administrators, and the division of labor between a Mr. Inside (president) and Mr. Outside (chairman), plausible as it looks on paper and in theory, rarely works out well in practice.

Greenleaf also argues for a separate professional staff for the trustees. This would be a relief to the president's office which often has a hard time providing adequate service to the trustees. It raises, however, delicate questions of cost, of the competence of the special staff, and of the relationship of trust between the trustees and the president. Staff work needs to be provided for trustees, but it should come out of an extended president's operations. Some chairmen may like to have an office of their own on campus where they can take care of their college or university duties. They run the danger, however, of becoming improperly embroiled in campus politics and management operations.

12. Role of the President

Good relations between the board and the president are central to a healthy institution. A strong board and a strong president will not always agree; that is to be expected. But constant conflict between the board and the president can be disastrous to the institution and according to one recent survey was the chief reason given for presidential resignations (Zwingle, 1981). The success of the relationship depends upon mutual understanding and hard work, for the relationship itself is a paradoxical one. The president is the agent of the board, its employee hired to carry out its policy mandates. At the same time the board looks, or ought to look, to the president for educational leadership.

In the community college field the president's position is somewhat more ambiguous. In an interesting examination of community college problems, Pray (1975) points to their traditionally close ties with local communities and school districts. He speculates on the satisfactions and frustrations which presidents feel as a result of their origin. Pray writes:

> *The community college president, some might say, lives in a sort of never-never land between the kind of immediacy of every problem faced in the role of a superintendent of schools and that of president of the four-year institution. To the extent that he is perceived as a glorified school superintendent, he is deprived of the supporting prestige which is an asset of the college presidency. To the extent that he assumes the style of the presidency of a more conventional or traditional college or university, he shuts himself away to a degree from the kind of thinking, philosophy and involvements which reflect the special nature of his institution (p.19).*

The most important aspects of the board/president relationship would include the following five:

1. A strong and effective board should be able to choose a strong and effective president. A rapid turnover of presidents is a sure sign of a weak, uncertain or divided board.

2. An effective board is one that delegates responsibility for administration to the president and is prepared to concentrate its attention on

86

policy issues. The distinction is not easy to draw in all cases and is therefore not always drawn (Cleary, 1979; Wood, 1982, chapter 15), but presidents and boards need to have a working understanding of their respective areas of responsibility. In the Research Triangle Institute survey 97 percent of the trustees indicated that the recommendations of the president were a factor in the decision-making process, by far the largest percentage for any of the nine factors listed. We have noted that the origin of community colleges tended to involve board members more actively in administrative matters, and the statement by Pray above would seem to bear this out. On the other hand, Drake found in the most recent survey of two-year institutions (1977) that over 90 percent of chairmen and presidents of both public and private colleges agreed with the proposition that the board had made a distinction between setting policy and administering the institution.

3. Institutions will not thrive unless the board has confidence in the president. The status of the president is likely to fluctuate among different constituencies and even within the same constituency. Faculty and students, board and alumni, will on the occasion of some decision of which they disapprove take a dim view of the president and his or her judgment, only to reverse themselves later on when new developments call for new decisions. The confidence of the board is of particular importance to the effectiveness of the president. They need to be open with one another, so that the president knows what the board expects and the board knows what the president expects. When president and board start playing politics with one another, openness and trust be-

gin to evaporate, and an effective working relationship disappears.

4. Confidence need not, indeed must not, be blind. "Today no board of trustees," writes Frantzreb (1974) "can afford the luxury of appointing a chief executive officer, then sitting back to see how he runs the institution.... The board must assure itself through its own mechanisms that its policies are being carried out through sound management. The board may delegate authority to manage; it cannot delegate responsibility" (p.8). How the board goes about monitoring the management of the institution is a delicate and complex matter, and a variety of methods have been tried (Nason, 1980). The purpose is not primarily to check up on the president, but to see how his or her work can best be supported and strengthened.

5. The president is leader and, as we saw in an earlier section, he or she is also the educator of the board. The president is after all a professional who is thinking about the institution's problems all the time. This presents another facet to the paradoxical relation between president and board. He or she is hired to do the board's bidding and at the same time to help its members understand the issues and reach sensible decisions. About all one can say is that with reasonable good will on both sides it works. The key is communication—full communication, bad news as well as good, failures as well as successes. In the Research Triangle Institute survey just over one-third of the trustees indicated that to a considerable or moderate extent board operations had been handicapped by failure of the president to achieve effective communication.

Some presidents are less candid and communicative than desirable because they try to protect their turf or have become defensive about their performance. These signs of weakness can often be corrected by sympathetic board counseling and support. It is more difficult when the president becomes dominant and even domineering. A strong president to begin with can become uncomfortably strong-minded over a period of time. In a sense this is an occupational disease into which presidents with long tenure in office are liable to fall unless on their guard. Since they know more than any of the trustees, have appointed virtually all the faculty, are idolized by many generations of students, they are sure they know the answers and with age comes impatience with the slow processes of consultation and explanation. Such presidents can dominate the system, including the board, whose members tend to become the proverbial rubber stamps. The college or university may have a mangificent administration, but it is likely to be left with a board unaccustomed to meeting its proper responsibilities and faced with real problems in picking up the pieces.

Should the president be a voting member of the governing board? Some are and some are not. The argument for making presidents members of the board is the status it gives them. Since the common complaint of presidents is that they lack the authority necessary to carry out their responsibilities, any device which will enhance that authority would seem desirable. But presidents are the hired agents of the board to whom the board delegates the authority to run the institution. They are accountable to the board, and as such, it is argued, they should not be members.

Logic would suggest that they not be voting members. To serve *ex officio* and without vote would be one way of combining status with logic. Boards should not meet, except for special executive sessions to review the president's performance and salary, without the president present. If the president is competent and if he or she can count on participating in board decisions, it probably makes no great difference whether the president is or is not a member.

13. Audit and Review

A thoughtful commentator has proposed the following bylaw for all college governing boards (Pray, 1974):

Audit and Review. *There shall be a periodic audit and review of the state of each of the following aspects of the College: (a) the work of the President, and of his administration; (b) the educational program, including faculty and student affairs; (c) business and physical plant management; (d) development and financing; (e) the Board of Trustees' operations and effectiveness. Each of these aspects shall be examined at least once every five years and one shall be conducted each year. These audits and reviews shall be conducted by ad hoc committees which shall report to the full board. The Chairman of such committees shall be a trustee.*

Does it not make sense? The burden of this study has been the high responsibility of trustees for the entire institution and its operations. That responsibility could well prompt thoughtful trustees to ask themselves the following questions: Have we a clear understanding of our legal, moral and social responsibilities as trustees? Are we the best possible board for this college or university; and if not, how do we become so? Are we spending our time on the right issues? Are we organized to be effective?

Assessment of the administration was discussed briefly in the preceding section. Assessment of the educational program and long range goals was explored in earlier sections of this chapter. What about self-assessment? Ought not boards to take a critical look at their own operations? There are many ways of doing this. Paltridge and Zwingle have useful chapters in the *Handbook* (Ingram, 1980). AGB has available self-study criteria for all types of boards. In addition, the AGB Board-Mentor Service further elaborates on this self-study procedure with the help of peer trustees and regents who bring a measure of objectivity to key issues of concern to all.

There is as much reason for boards to review their own status, composition and operations as to review other components of the institution. A steadily increasing number of governing boards are doing so. After all, responsibility, like charity, begins at home.

14. Board Morale

The business of being a college or university trustee makes extraordinary demands on the men and women who serve in that capacity. It is hard work. It demands time. It has been honored all too often with public criticism and disparagement. Why are 38,000 busy men and women willing to volunteer their services?

If one is an alumnus or alumna of the college or an active member of the church to which the college is related, there is the strong pull of loyalty or affection or both. For many trustees prestige is a significant element. There is pleasure in being on the inside, in the know, and in being associated with people whom one respects. In our society we think of trustees as important people, sometimes as powerful ones.

There are, however, other reasons less centered in self. It is good to be identified with something bigger than oneself. Most people have some concern for the public good, and many are willing to serve it at some personal sacrifice. There is an exhilaration in coping constructively with others in solving difficult problems, of which education is currently providing its full share. "However a man feels about his work," wrote the late Justice Oliver Wendell Holmes 50 years ago, "nature is likely to see to it that his business becomes his master and an end in itself, so that he may find that he has been a martyr under the illusion of self seeking. But we rank men partly at least by the nature of their dominant interest, and we think more highly of those who are conscious of ulterior ends—be those ends intellectual ideals, to see the universal in the particular, or the sympathetic wish to help their kind."[21]

The effective board will have a sense of purpose, an awareness of working for something larger and more important than merely the interests of the individuals who compose the board. Moments of deep concern, of anxiety over what may happen, should be followed by periods of elation, of genuine satisfaction, of joy. Where boards are working well, members enjoy each other, the give and take of argument, the common commitment. They leave the meetings with a certain exhilara-

21. From an unpublished letter to The Honorable Charles E. Wyzanski, Jr., Senior District Judge (Retired) in the U.S. District Court for the District of Massachusetts.

tion as a result of the ideas and issues and decisions in which they participated. They look forward to the next with pleasant anticipation. (See Wood, 1982, pp. 144-46).

And why not? No country has made such an investment in higher education as has the United States. No country has provided so many and such diverse kinds of postsecondary institutions as the United States. To be a part of such an enterprise is to be involved in a significant way in the action of our time.

TRUSTEES AND THE LAW

A....board member, who has voluntarily undertaken the task of supervising the operation of the school and the activities of the students, must be held to a standard of conduct based not only on permissible intentions, but also on knowledge of the basic unquestioned constitutional rights of his charges.

Justice Byron R. White

94

Chapter 1 reviewed the various forces which, since World War II, have transformed the classic collegial model of governance with its emphasis on informal methods of arriving at consensus into a politicized pattern of confrontation with emphasis on formal rights and recourse to the courts to settle what had formerly been considered the private business of academia. The change in temper or climate is well documented by the proliferation in the last few years of legal suits involving colleges and universities.

Legal Liability of Trustees

Until very recently the trustees of colleges and universities were considered to be largely immune to outside interference. Their decisions, and the actions of administrators and faculty in accordance with those decisions, were viewed as a private matter for which they were not accountable in courts of law. That has now changed. "Trustees can no longer take comfort in the proposition that if they exercise ordinary and reasonable care in the performance of their duties, exhibiting honesty and good faith, they can avoid lawsuits and the risk of personal liability" (AGB, Ad Hoc Committee, 1982, p. 1).

Justice White's statement in 1975 in the case of *Wood v. Strickland* is a warning to trustees that they should be aware of the "unquestioned constitutional rights" of students and faculty and should act accordingly.[1] Those rights are set forth, in part, in the 14th Amendment which states: "No state shall abridge the privileges or immunities of citizens of the United States, nor shall any state deprive any person of life, liberty or property without due process of law."

1. In this section I am indebted to Bruce E. Woodruff and his excellent article, "Trustees Must Know the Law," in AGB Reports, Nov./Dec. 1976.

The Civil Rights Act of 1871, passed in the aftermath of the Civil War and frequently called the Ku Klux Klan Act, provided that any person who deprived another of any rights should "be liable to the party injured for redress." For a hundred years this Act was considered inapplicable to colleges and universities. Since 1975, however, it has been frequently used as the legal grounds for damages against institutions, their officers and trustees by aggrieved parties who thought their rights abridged.

Further grounds for legal suits are to be found in the Equal Employment Opportunity Act of 1972 which requires every college and university receiving federal funds to follow affirmative action guidelines; in Title IX of the Educational Amendment Act of 1972 which prohibits sex discrimination in facilities, athletics, financial aid and the like; in the Educational Rights and Privacy Act of 1974 (the Buckley Amendment) giving students access to their college records and limiting their availability to others (such as potential employers) without express permission from the students; in Section 504 of the Rehabilitation Act of 1973 requiring special facilities for the handicapped.

Both students and faculty have become well aware of their constitutional rights and have shown no reluctance to go to court to get them enforced. Faculty members without tenure who are not reappointed or who are denied tenure are quick to claim discrimination on grounds of race or sex or some form of prejudice. Students have brought suit on grounds of censorship of publications, of discrimination against organizations such as gay student groups, of improper disciplinary decisions, even of improper academic treatment. Courts have not been inclined to get involved in strictly academic issues, such as complaints over grades or academic standing, but they have increasingly accepted jurisdiction on other grounds. The education pages of many newspapers report such cases, and every issue of *The Chronicle of Higher Education* carries one or more stories.

In view of the legal temper of the time it is important that trustees not only know what is legally permissible and what is not,[2] but also that they establish, or insist that there be established, codes of student conduct and procedures for faculty appointments, promotions and tenure, which will insure due process. These codes and regulations should be in writing. They should be impartially applied. The board must be prepared to serve, if necessary, as a court of appeal. They need to make sure that performance lives up to the promise in promotional literature (Stark, 1975).

Conflicts of Interest

An important and troublesome aspect of the legal liability of trustees stems from conflicts of interest. "A conflict may arise," write Lascell and Hallenbeck, "whenever a college or university trustee has or represents interests that could compete with the interests of the institution that the trustee serves."[3] Conflicts resulting in personal gain from doing business with the institution are obvious to most trustees. But there are other and subtler conflicts involving gifts to the institution, decisions with respect to endowment, the solicitation of gifts where the individual is a trustee of two or more boards. The fiduciary responsibility of trustees is one of full loyalty to the institution,

2. For example, in cases involving public institutions (and the same may be applicable to private ones) courts have ruled that students may not be deprived of their rights of free speech, of assembly and of the press. "In like manner, censorship of student publications in the absence of a showing of material disruption or obscenity has been held an unwarranted interference with protected First Amendment rights. Nor does the fact that the college finances the publication affect its obligation to refrain from infringing on the free speech rights of the student editors" (Woodruff, 1976, pp.14-15).

3. Their chapter, "Contending with Conflicts of Interest and Liability," in the Handbook of College and University Trusteeship is recommended to all trustees (Ingram, 1980).

and this means that its interests must always be paramount. The potential conflicts of interest for faculty or students serving as trustees of the institution of which they are members was discussed in the preceding chapter.

Conflict relates not only to the individual trustee, but also to his or her family and associates. Sometimes the connection or situation seems remote, more theoretical than actual; but trustees need to keep in mind that society has become more sensitive to potential conflicts of interest and more determined to reduce them. A spate of statutes and administrative regulations has been created for just this purpose.

The most widely discussed and probably the most influential case in this area is *Stern v. Lucy Webb Hayes National Training School,* better known as the Sibley Hospital case. In essence, suit was brought against certain trustees of the hospital (among others) on grounds that they had sought to enrich themselves by depositing money belonging to the hospital in banks of which they were directors and by employing investment counsel in which one of the trustees was personally involved to manage the hospital's endowment. The suit further charged that the trustees had failed in their fiduciary responsibilities by absenting themselves from board meetings at which important decisions were taken and by failing to convene for a long period of time the financial committee which was presumed to oversee investments.

Judge Gesell of the Federal District Court in the District of Columbia absolved the defendants of enriching themselves at the expense of the hospital, but found them guilty of failing in their fiduciary duty of care and loyalty to the hospital.

More specifically, he found that each of the defendant trustees had breached his fiduciary responsibility in that:

1. [He] *failed to use due diligence in supervising the actions of those officers, employees or outside experts to whom the responsibility for making day-to-day financial investment decisions has been delegated.*

2. *He knowingly permitted the hospital to enter into a business transaction with himself...without having previously informed the persons charged with approving that transaction of his interest or position.*

3. *He actively participated in or voted in favor of a decision by the board or any committee....thereof to transact business with himself....*

4. *He otherwise failed to perform his duties honestly, in good faith, and with a reasonable amount of diligence and care* (Mace, 1976).

Judge Gesell imposed no monetary penalties, but did set requirements some of which have become part of what is now recommended as standard procedure. He required that the trustees and officers draft a written program for the investment of the hospital's available funds, that the entire board review all funds to be sure they were invested in accordance with the statement, that each trustee file in writing with the board a full listing of all affiliations with any financial institution doing business with the hospital, that the treasurer and auditors make and report special reviews of business transactions involving any connection with a trustee, and that each current trustee and all new trustees over the following five years file in writing a statement that they had read the court's opinion.

Many colleges and universities are now establishing written policies regarding conflicts of interest and are requiring all trustees to file with an appropriate officer or designated trustee a list of relationships with financial institutions and such non-profit organizations as might present a potential conflict, together with a roster of family members and associates whose connections might also create conflicts of interest. The Association of Governing Boards has adopted a statement on conflict of interest which can be found in Resource D at the end of the trusteeship *Handbook* (Ingram, 1980), together with sample record forms and disclosure letters.

Liability Protection

With the increasing cost of litigation and with the threat of substantial damages being awarded against individual officers and trustees, as in the *Endress* case,[4] trustees are naturally concerned about ways of protecting themselves. In most states the law permits the institution to indemnify trustees for the expense of lawsuits and costs of settlement, but the statutes vary from one state to another and the costs of indemnification may be damaging, if not prohibitive, to colleges and universities operating close to the margin of solvency.

One form of protection is liability insurance, normally carried by the institution on behalf of its officers and trustees, but also available to individual trustees as well. Liability insurance is a complicated and technical business with wide

4. *Patricia Endress was summarily fired from her position on the faculty of Brookdale Community College (N.J.) for writing an editorial in the school paper criticizing the chairman of the board. The New Jersey Superior Court found punitive damages against the president and six trustees. The case was appealed to the New Jersey Appellate Division. "Governing board members can take little solace is the appellate decision. While the court narrowly reversed the award of punitive damages against the board members, primarily because of the new and unsettled nature of the constitutional issues, it provided future plaintiffs with a blueprint for proving their cases. In addition, punitive damages were awarded against the college president and at least a portion of the compensatory award was awarded against all defendants." (Woodruff, 1976, pp.16-7).*

100

variations in coverage, in terms of renewal, in exceptions and exclusions. Premiums tend to run high, and only a few companies provide this kind of protection. The brief report, *Trustee Liability Insurance*, published in 1982 by the Association of Governing Boards Ad Hoc Committee, gives the best overall view of the subject[5]

Lascell and Hallenbeck make the comforting observation that "although there are thousands of colleges, universities, museums, and other charitable corporations in the country, the reported number of money judgments finally obtained against individual trustees is insignificant, at least of today." (Ingram, 1980, p.361) Even so, it is wise to take the kind of precautions which obviate the likelihood of adverse judgments. Woodruff suggests seven rules (1976, p.18):

1. *Avoid precipitous action (don't lose your cool).*
2. *Make sure you have all the facts. Don't rely only on one side's version of a disputed issue— demand sufficient information before voting.*
3. *Remember your duty is to the institution you serve, not to any individual member of the administration.*
4. *Follow the rules—the board or college policies and procedures that have been written down.*
5. *Make an effort to attend every board meeting. (By being chronically absent, you may incur liability.)*
6. *When in doubt, consult your president, chancellor, and counsel—in other words, use your paid professionals.*
7. *Avoid conflicts of interest by disclosing potential conflict and refusing to debate, discuss or vote with respect to any matter in which you or your family have an interest. (1976, p.18)*

5. The most complete coverage is to be found in Aiken, Adams and Hall, Liability (1976)—an analysis of "Legal Liabilities in Higher Education: Their Scope and Management."

APPENDIX A
Characteristics of
Governing Boards

Characteristics of Voting Members of Governing Boards
(In Percentages)

Characteristic	Total Governing Boards				Public			Private	
	Total (N=2,314)	Single-Campus (N=2,150)	Multi-Campus ≤3 (N=92)	Multi-Campus ≥3 (N=72)	Single-Campus (N=632)	Multi-Campus ≤3 (N=71)	Multi-Campus ≥3 (N=67)	Single-Campus (N=1,518)	Multi-Campus (N=26)
Number of voting members	47,138	44,759	1,368	1,011	5,458	609	846	39,301	924
Sex:									
Men	84.9	84.9	85.8	85.2	81.7	84.9	84.1	85.3	87.3
Women	15.1	15.1	14.2	14.8	18.3	15.1	15.9	14.7	12.7
Total	100.0	100.0	100.0	100.0	100.0	100.0	100.0	100.0	100.0
Race:									
Black	6.0	5.9	4.5	8.7	10.9	6.7	9.7	5.2	2.9
Other minority	1.0	1.0	1.2	2.4	2.7	2.1	2.9	.7	.3
White	93.0	93.1	94.3	88.9	86.4	91.1	87.4	94.0	96.8
Total	100.0	100.0	100.0	100.0	100.0	100.0	100.0	100.0	100.0
Education:									
Less than high school	.4	.3	.1	4.5	.7	.3	5.4	.3	0
High school diploma	6.5	6.5	7.8	5.8	11.8	8.5	6.9	5.8	5.9
A.A., A.S.	2.8	2.8	1.6	3.6	4.8	3.1	3.9	2.5	.7
B.A., B.S.	38.8	38.8	40.3	35.8	37.7	38.6	38.0	38.9	38.4
M.A., M.S., M.A.T.	19.4	19.6	14.7	16.8	17.5	15.8	15.1	19.8	16.0
Ph.D., Ed.D.	11.0	11.1	10.1	8.3	5.9	5.2	6.7	11.8	14.6
M.D., J.D.	21.2	21.0	25.3	25.2	21.6	28.4	24.0	20.9	24.3
Total	100.0	100.0	100.0	100.0	100.0	100.0	100.0	100.0	100.0
Age:									
Less than 30 years old	2.2	2.1	2.9	4.6	2.2	3.0	5.5	2.1	2.3
20-39 years old	7.3	7.3	5.3	7.4	9.6	7.4	8.9	7.0	3.0
40-49 years old	24.4	24.3	24.6	25.0	32.9	25.1	27.2	23.2	22.4
50-59 years old	35.0	34.9	39.0	34.4	33.7	41.1	34.0	35.0	37.1
60-69 years old	24.7	24.8	23.5	22.9	16.9	18.4	18.8	25.8	30.5
70 years old or older	6.5	6.6	4.7	5.7	4.6	5.0	5.6	6.8	4.7
Total	100.0	100.0	100.0	100.0	100.0	100.0	100.0	100.0	100.0

Characteristics of Voting Members of Single-Campus Governing Boards
(In Percentages)

Characteristics	Public Single-Campus Boards			Private Single-Campus Boards		
	University (N=27)	Four-Year (N=114)	Two-Year (N=491)	University (N=68)	Four-Year (N=1,217)	Two-Year (N=233)
Number of voting members	360	1,347	3,751	2,338	31,848	5,115
Sex:						
Men	87.4	84.0	80.4	89.9	87.3	71.1
Women	12.6	16.0	19.6	10.1	12.7	28.9
Total	100.0	100.0	100.0	100.0	100.0	100.0
Race:						
Black	5.6	24.9	6.4	3.7	5.1	6.5
Other minority	2.0	2.2	3.0	.3	.8	.5
White	92.5	72.9	90.6	96.0	94.1	92.9
Total	100.0	100.0	100.0	100.0	100.0	100.0
Education:						
Less than high school	0	.2	.9	*	.3	.3
High school diploma	10.2	10.2	12.6	4.8	6.2	3.3
A.A., A.S.	.8	.7	6.8	1.2	2.0	6.2
B.A., B.S.	41.8	31.6	39.6	39.6	39.2	37.3
M.A., M.S., M.A.T.	9.0	16.4	18.7	15.5	18.6	29.7
Ph.D., Ed.D.	5.1	8.9	4.9	13.7	12.2	8.1
M.D., J.D.	33.1	32.0	16.7	25.2	21.5	15.1
Total	100.0	100.0	100.0	100.0	-100.0	100.0
Age:						
Less than 30 years old	2.5	3.3	1.9	1.6	2.2	1.4
20-39 years old	6.9	9.3	10.0	4.2	7.0	8.6
40-49 years old	17.6	31.0	34.9	15.2	24.0	21.9
50-59 years old	40.7	33.4	33.2	35.5	34.8	35.9
60-69 years old	25.3	18.3	15.7	31.9	25.3	26.3
70 years old or older	7.1	4.7	4.3	11.6	6.6	5.9
Total	100.0	100.0	100.0	100.0	100.0	100.0

*Less than .05 percent.

Characteristics of Voting Members of Single-Campus Governing Boards
(In Percentages)

Primary Occupation	Public Single-Campus Boards			Private Single-Campus Boards		
	University (N = 27)	Four-Year (N = 114)	Two-Year (N = 491)	University (N = 68)	Four-Year (N = 1,217))	Two-Year (N = 233)
Number of voting members	360	1,347	3,751	2,338	31,848	5,115
Business:						
Executive, mining and manufacturing firm	18.8	16.6	21.2	29.2	20.6	16.7
Executive, banking firm	14.5	9.4	8.8	16.1	11.4	8.2
Other	4.3	3.0	5.0	2.8	2.9	1.9
Education:						
Officer, higher education	2.0	2.3	2.3	5.8	6.3	7.4
Faculty, higher education	.9	4.4	2.1	2.8	3.4	4.2
Student	1.2	1.7	.7	1.9	1.1	.0
Teacher or administrator, primary or secondary school	1.4	4.5	4.3	.8	2.1	6.7
Other	1.7	1.1	.8	.4	.4	2.0
Professional services:						
Clergy	.3	.7	1.0	5.0	11.8	14.8
Lawyer	18.2	18.4	9.3	10.8	7.7	6.9
Doctor, dentist	6.1	7.5	6.0	2.0	6.0	3.6
Other	1.4	1.7	1.9	1.1	1.0	.3
Other:						
Executive, nonprofit organization	2.0	3.2	2.4	3.2	4.5	4.0
Farmer	2.9	3.0	3.6	.4	.9	.3
Homemaker	5.5	9.0	8.9	3.1	4.1	8.1
Retired	7.2	6.6	9.7	8.9	9.2	9.8
Other	11.6	7.1	12.0	5.6	6.7	5.2
Total	100.0	100.0	100.0	100.0	100.0	100.0

Primary Occupation of Voting Members of Governing Boards
(In Percentages)

Characteristic	Total Governing Boards				Public			Private	
	Total (N = 2,314)	Single-Campus (N = 2,150)	Multi-Campus ≤3 (N = 92)	Multi-Campus >3 (N = 72)	Single-Campus (N = 632)	Multi-Campus ≤3 (N = 71)	Multi-Campus >3 (N = 67)	Single-Campus (N = 1,518)	Multi-Campus (N = 26)
Number of voting members	47,138	44,759	1,368	1,011	5,458	609	846	39,301	924
Business:									
Executive, mining and manufacturing firm	20.3	20.5	17.8	15.3	20.2	12.4	14.3	20.6	21.8
Executive, banking firm	11.2	11.0	14.8	12.3	9.3	13.5	9.6	11.2	17.5
Other	3.0	2.9	3.3	3.6	4.6	3.0	4.0	2.7	3.2
Education:									
Officer, higher education	5.9	5.9	4.0	6.1	2.3	.2	3.6	6.4	9.1
Faculty, higher education	3.3	3.3	2.9	2.0	2.5	1.0	2.0	3.5	3.9
Student	1.0	1.0	1.5	3.2	.9	1.3	3.8	1.0	1.3
Teacher or administrator, primary or secondary school	2.9	2.8	3.0	3.7	4.2	4.8	4.4	2.7	1.3
Other	.7	.7	2.0	1.6	.9	3.1	1.9	.6	1.0
Professional services:									
Clergy	10.1	10.5	1.3	.8	.9	.5	.6	11.8	1.9
Lawyer	8.4	8.2	12.2	12.5	11.7	14.2	13.3	7.7	10.3
Doctor, dentist	5.5	5.6	3.1	6.5	6.3	4.5	7.1	5.5	2.3
Other	1.1	1.0	1.7	2.7	1.8	2.8	2.9	.9	1.0
Other:									
Executive, nonprofit organization	4.1	4.2	3.5	3.6	2.5	3.5	3.7	4.4	3.4
Farmer	1.3	1.1	3.6	5.5	3.4	7.6	6.0	.8	.9
Homemaker	5.0	5.0	5.4	3.7	8.7	7.3	4.4	4.5	3.2
Retired	9.1	9.2	8.0	5.0	8.9	7.6	5.4	9.2	7.3
Other	7.2	7.0	12.1	12.1	11.0	11.9	12.9	6.5	10.7
Total	100.0	100.0	100.0	100.0	100.0	100.0	100.0	100.0	100.0

APPENDIX B
Bibliography

Aiken, Roy J., Adams, John F., Hall, John W. *Liability—Legal Liabilities in Higher Education: Their Scope and Management.* Washington, D.C., Association of American Colleges, 1976.

Angell, Daniel "How to Play the State Capitol Game." *AGB Reports*, Vol. 22 No. 5, September/October 1980.

Ashby, Eric, *Any Person, Any Study: An Essay on Higher Education in the United States.* New York: McGraw-Hill, 1971.

Association of Governing Boards of Universities and Colleges, National Commission on College and University Trustee Selection. *Recommendations for Improving Trustee Selection in Private Colleges and Universities.* Washington: Association of Governing Boards, 1980.

Association of Governing Boards of Universities and Colleges, National Commission on College and University Trustee Selection. *Recommendations for Improving Trustee Selection in Public Colleges and Universities.* Washington: Association of Governing Boards, 1980.

Association of Governing Boards. *Trustee Liability Insurance.* Washington, D.C.: AGB, 1982.

Association of Governing Boards Ad Hoc Committee. *Trustee Liability Insurance.* Washington: Association of Governing Boards, 1982.

Association of Governing Boards and National Association of College and University Business Officers. *Financial Responsibilities of Governing Boards of Colleges and Universities.* Washington: AGB & NACUBO, 1979.

Bailey, Stephen K. *"A Comparison of the University With a Government Bureau."* In J. A. Perkins (Ed.), *The University as an Organization.* New York: McGraw-Hill, 1973.

Balderston, F. E. *Managing Today's University.* San Francisco: Jossey-Bass, 1974.

Balderidge, J. R., and others. *Policy Making and Effective Leadership.* San Francisco: Jossey-Bass, 1978.

Bean, Atherton. *"The Liberal Arts College Trustee's Next 25 Years." AGB Reports,* Vol. 17, No. 3, May/June 1975.

Bell, Laird. *"From the Trustees' Corner."* Association of American Colleges Bulletin, 42 (3), 1956.

Bowen, H. R. *Investment in Learning—The Individual and Social Value of American Higher Education.* San Francisco: Jossey-Bass, 1977.

Bowen, Otis R. *"An Agenda for Statewide Boards." AGB Reports,* Vol. 21, No. 6, November/December 1979.

Calkins, Hugh. *"A Plan for Survival." AGB Reports,* Vol. 17, No. 4, January/February 1975.

Carnegie Commission on Higher Education. *Governance of Higher Education: Six Priority Problems.* New York: McGraw-Hill, 1973.

Carnegie Commission on Higher Education. *The Purposes and Performances of Higher Education in the United States,* Report and Recommendations. New York: McGraw-Hill, 1973.

Carnegie Council on Policy Studies in Higher Education. *Three Thousand Futures.* San Francisco: Jossey-Bass, 1980.

Carnegie Foundation for Advancement of Teaching, *More Than Survival.* San Francisco: McGraw-Hill, 1975.

Clark, B. R. and Youn, T. J. K. *Academic Power in the United States.* ERIC/Higher Education Research Report, No. 3. Washington: American Association for Higher Education, 1976.

Davis, J. S. and Batchelor, S. A. *The Elective.* Cleary, R. E. *"Who's in Charge Here?" AGB Reports,* Vol. 21, No. 6, November/December 1979.

Cohen, M. D. and March, J. G. *Leadership and Ambiguity—The American College President.* New York: McGraw-Hill, 1974.

Coolidge, C. A. *"How to Be a Good Fellow." Harvard Alumni Bulletin,* 58 (8), 1956. Pp. 350-352, 360.

Corson, John J. *The Governance of Colleges and Universities* (revised edition). New York: McGraw-Hill, 1975.

Council for the Advancement of Small Colleges (Pub.). *The Trustee.* Washington: CASC, undated.

Cowley, W.H. *Presidents, Professors, and Trustees.* San Francisco: Jossey-Bass, 1980.

Davis, J.S. and Batchelor, S.A. *The Effective College and University Board: A Report of a National Survey of Trustees and Presidents.* Research Triangle Park, N.C.: Research Triangle Institute, 1974.

Dobbins, C.G. and Lee, C.B.T. (Ed.). *Whose Goals for American Higher Education?* Washington: American Council on Eduction, 1968.

Dodds, H.W. *The Academic President — Educator or Caretaker?* New York: McGraw-Hill, 1962.

Drake, S.L. *Research Report: A Study of Community and Junior College Boards of Trustees.* Washington: Association of Community and Junior Colleges, 1977.

Dressel, P.L. and Fairay, W.H. *Return to Responsibility — Constraints on Autonomy in Higher Education.* San Francisco: Jossey-Bass, 1972.

Dunseath, J.E. "Open Meetings — a Threat to Effective Governance." Transcript of speech delivered to students and faculty at University of Arizona, 1970.

Duryea, E.D. "Evolution of University Organization." In J.A. Perkins (Ed.), *The University as an Organization.* New York: McGraw-Hill, 1973.

Enarson, H.L. "The Occasional Search for the Public Interest." *AGB Reports,* Vol. 17, No. 2, March/April 1975.

Epstein, L.D. *Governing the University — The Campus and the Public Interest.* San Francisco: Jossey-Bass, 1974.

Fleming, R.W. "Governing Boards in Major Public Institutions." *AGB Reports,* Vol. 17, No. 6, November/December 1975.

Frantzreb, A.C. *Operational Imperatives for a College Board of Trustees in the 1970s.* Arlington, VA.: Frantzreb and Pray Associates, 1970.

Frantzreb, A.C. "Secrets of a Board Chairman." 1974.

Frantzreb, A.C. (Ed.), New Directions for Institutional Advancement: No. 14. *Trustee's Role in Advancement.* San Francisco: Jossey-Bass, 1981.

Gale, R.L. "Selecting and Deploying Trustees." In R.T. Ingram's (Ed.) *Handbook of College and University Trusteeship.* San Francisco: Jossey-Bass, 1980.

Glenny, L. A., Berdahl, R. O. Palola, E. G., Paltridge, J. G. *Coordinating Higher Education for the '70s — Multi-campus and Statewide Guidelines for Practice.* Berkeley, CA.: Center for Research and Development in Higher Education, 1971.

Gomberg, I. L. and Atelsek, F. J. *Composition of College and University Governing Boards,* Higher Education Panel Report No. 35. Washington: American Council on Education, 1977.

Gomberg, I. L. and Atelsek, F. J. "Who's on the Board?" *AGB Reports,* Vol. 19, No. 6, November/December 1977.

Greenleaf, Robert K. "The Trustee: The Buck Starts Here." *Foundation News.* July/August 1973.

Greenleaf, R. K. *Trustees As Servants.* Cambridge, Mass.: Center for Applied Studies, 1974.

Hartnett, R. T. *College and University Trustees: Their Backgrounds, Roles and Educational Attitudes.* Princeton, N. J.: Educational Testing Service, 1969.

Heilbron, L. H. *The College and University Trustee — A View from the Board Room.* San Francisco: Jossey-Bass, 1973.

Henderson, A. D. *The Role of the Governing Board.* Washington: Association of Governing Boards, 1967.

Hodgkinson, H. L. *Campus Governance: The Amazing Thing Is That It Woks At All.* Report 11. Washington: ERIC Clearinghouse on Higher Education, 1971.

Houle, C. O. *The Effective Board.* New York: The Association Press, 1960.

Hyde, R. M. "Why Don't Trustees Discuss Government?" *AGB Reports,* Vol. 19, No. 1, January/February 1977.

Ingram, R. T. (Ed.) *Handbook of College and University Trusteeship.* San Francisco: Jossey-Bass, 1980.

Ingram, R. T. "Assuming Trustee Orientation and Development." In R. T. Ingram's (Ed.) *Handbook of College and University Trusteeship.* San Francisco: Jossey-Bass, 1980.

Ingram, R. T. "Trusteeship in the Church-Related College in the '80s." *Current Issues in Catholic Higher Education,* 2 (1), 1981.

Jencks, D. and Riesman, D. *The Academic Revolution.* New York: Doubleday, 1968.

Jenny, H. H. and Associates. *Hang-Gliding or Looking for an Updraft: A Study of College and University Finance in the 1980s — The Capital Margin.* Wooster, Ohio and Boulder, Colorado: The College of Wooster and John Minter Associates, Inc., 1981.

Kauffman, J. F. *At The Pleasure of the Board.*
Washington: American Council on
Education, 1980.

Kauffman, J. F. *The Selection of College and
University Presidents.* Washington:
Association of American Colleges, 1974.

Kerr, Clark, *The Uses of the University.*
Cambridge, Mass.: Harvard University
Press, 1963.

Kerr, Clark, "The Trustee Faces Steady
State." *AGB Reports,* Vol. 17, No. 3,
May/June 1975.

Kerr, Clark, "Opportunities and Dangers."
AGB Reports, Vol. 21, No. 1,
January/February 1979.

King, M. C. and Brender, R. L.
*President-Trustee Relationships: Meeting
the Challenge of Leadership.* Washington:
American Association of Community and
Junior Colleges, 1977.

Krusden, J. K. "The Trustee Management
Committee." In A. C. Frantzreb (Ed.),
Trustee's Role in Advancement. San Francisco:
Jossey-Bass, 1981.

Lascell, David M. and Hallenbeck, A. M.
"Contending With Conflicts of Interest and
Liability." In R. T. Ingram (Ed.),
*Handbook of College and University
Trusteeship.* San Francisco: Jossey-Bass, 1980.

Lavine, John M. "The Value of a Single
System." *AGB Reports,* Vol. 22, No. 1,
January/February 1980.

Lee, E. C. and Bowen, F. M. "Governing
Boards in Multicampus Universities."
AGB Reports, Vol. 14, No. 2, March 1972.

Mace, M. L. "Standards of Care for
Trustees." *Harvard Business Review,*
1976, 54 (1).

Manne, H. G. "The Political Economy of
Modern Universities." *AGB Reports,* Vol. 15,
No. 5, October 1972.

Mayhew, L. B. *Surviving the Eighties.*
San Francisco: Jossey-Bass, 1980.

Millett, J. D. *Management, Governance and
Leadership: A Guide for College and
University Administrators.* New York:
Amacom, 1980.

Millett, J.D. *New Structures of Campus Power.*
San Francisco: Jossey-Bass, 1978.

Millett, J.D. "What, No Governing Boards?"
AGB Reports, Vol. 17, No. 6,
November/December 1975.

Mills, P. K. "Community College Trustees:
A Survey." *The Two-Year College Trustee:
National Issues and Perspectives.* Washington:
Association of Governing Boards, 1972.

Mortimer, K. P. and McConnell, T. R. *Sharing Authority Effectively.* San Francisco: Jossey-Bass, 1978.

Munitz, B. "Memo to a Multicampus Trustee …from a Flagship CEO." *AGB Reports,* Vol. 23, No. 5, September/October 1981.

Munitz, B. "Reviewing Presidential Leadership." In R.T. Ingram's (Ed.), *Handbook of College and University Trusteeship.* San Francisco: Jossey-Bass, 1980.

Nabrit, S.H. and Scott, Jr., J.S. *Inventory of Academic Leadership, an Analysis of the Boards of Trustees of Fifty Predominantly Negro Institutions.* Atlanta, GA.: Southern Fellowship Fund, 1968.

Nason, J.W. *Presidential Assessment.* Washington: Association of Governing Boards, 1980.

Nason, J.W. "Selecting the Chief Executive." In R.T. Ingram (Ed.), *Handbook of College and University Trusteeship.* San Francisco: Jossey-Bass, 1980.

Nelson, C.A. "Improving Your Meetings Four Ways." *AGB Reports,* Vol. 21, No. 5, September/October 1979.

Nelson, C.A. "Managing Resources." In R.T. Ingram (Ed.), *Handbook of College and University Trusteeship.* San Francisco: Jossey-Bass, 1980.

Nelson, C. A. and Turk, F. J. "Some Facts About Trustees." *AGB Reports,* Vol. 16, No. 2, April 1974.

Paltridge, J. G. "Folklore and Some Facts About Trustee Decisions." *AGB Reports,* Vol. 16, No. 6, March 1974.

Paltridge, J. G. "Studying Board Effectiveness." In R.T. Ingram (Ed.), *Handbook of College and University Trusteeship.* San Francisco: Jossey-Bass, 1980.

Paltridge, J. G., Hurst, J. and Morgan, A. *A Board of Trustees: Their Decision Patterns,* Berkeley, CA.: Center for Research and Development in Higher Education, 1973.

Parsonage, R. R. (Ed.). *Church Related Higher Education.* Valley Forge PA.: Judson Press, 1978.

Perkins, J. A. *The University in Transition.* Princeton, NJ: Princeton University Press, 1966.

Perkins, J. A. "Conflicting Responsibilities of Governing Boards." In J. A. Perkins (Ed.), *The University as an Organization.* New York: McGraw-Hill, 1973.

Perkins, J. A. (Ed.). *The University as an Organization.* New York: McGraw-Hill, 1973.

Perkins, J. A. (Ed.) and Israel, B. B. (Assoc. Ed.). *Higher Education: From Autonomy to Systems.* New York: International Council for Educational Development, 1972.

Pocock, J.W. "Reporting Finances." In R.T. Ingram (Ed.), *Handbook for College and University Trusteeship*, San Francisco: Jossey-Bass, 1980.

Posey, C.L. "The Things I've Unlearned." *AGM Reports*, Vol. 21, No. 6, November/December 1979.

Potter, G.E. *Trusteeship: Handbook for Community College and Technical Institute Trustees*. Washington: Association of Community College Trustees, 1979.

Pray, F.C. *A New Look at Community College Boards of Trustees and Presidents and Their Relationships*. Washington: American Association of Community and Junior Colleges, 1975.

Pray, F.C. "The State of the Art of College Trusteeship." Mimeographed. Arlington, VA.: Frantzreb and Pray Associates, 1974.

Pray, F.C. "Trusteeship for College and Universities." Brochure published by Council for Financial Aid to Education: New York, 1964.

Radock, M. and Jacobson, H.K. "Securing Resources." In R.T. Ingram (Ed.), *Handbook of College and University Trusteeship*. San Francisco: Jossey-Bass, 1980.

Rauh, M.A. *The Trusteeship of Colleges and Universities*. New York: McGraw-Hill, 1969.

Riesman, David. *On Higher Education: The Academic Enterprise in an Era of Rising Student Consumerism*. San Francisco: Jossey-Bass, 1980.

Riley, G.L. and Baldridge, J.V. (Ed). *Governing Academic Organizations: New Problems, New Perspectives*. Berkeley, CA.: McCutchan Publishing Corp., 1977.

Ruml, B. and Morrison, D.H. *Memo to a College Trustee*. New York: McGraw-Hill, 1959.

Scarlett, M. "Why Presidents Don't Like State Boards." *AGB Reports*, Vol. 22, No. 5, September/October 1980.

Smith, G.K. (Ed.), *Agony and Promise — Current Issues in Higher Education 1969*. San Francisco: Jossey-Bass, 1969.

Smith, G.K. (Ed.), *New Teaching, New Learning — Current Issues in Higher Education, 1971*. San Francisco: Jossey-Bass, 1971.

Stadtman, V.A. *Academic Adaptions, Higher Education Prepares for the 1980s and 1990s*. San Francisco: Jossey-Bass, 1980.

Stamm, M.J. "Emerging Corporate Models of Governance in Contemporary American Catholic Higher Education." *Current Issues in Catholic Higher Education*, 2(1), 1981.

Stark, J.S. "The Responsibility of Trustees in Relation to Consumer Protection." Address at Regents Eleventh Annual Trustee Conference. Albany, NY: State Education Department, 1975.

Stern, V. Lucy *Webb Hayes National Training School for Deaconesses and Missionaries*, et. al., 381, F. Supp. 1003 (D.D.C., 1974).

Sweet, D. L. "What's Wrong with State Boards." *AGB Reports*, Vol. 22, No. 1, January/February 1980.

Trow, M. "Reflections on the Transition from Mass to Universal Higher Education." *Daedalus*, 99 (1), 1970.

Trow, M. "The Public and Private Lives of Higher Education."*Daedalus*, 104 (1), 1975.

Veblen, T. *The Higher Learning in America* (1918). New York: Hill and Wang, 1957.

Walker, D. E. *The Effective Administrator.*, San Francisco: Jossey-Bass, 1979.

Whitehead, A. N. *The Aims of Education and Other Essays* (1929). New York: The New American Library, 1949.

Wicke, M. F. *Handbook for Trustees of Church-Related Colleges and Universities*. Nashville, TN: Board of Education, The Methodist Church, 1957.

Williams, G. D. "And Who's on the State Board?" *AGB Reports*, Vol. 19, No. 6, November/December 1977.

Wilson, L. (Ed.). *Emerging Patterns in American Higher Education*. Washington: American Council on Education, 1965.

Wise, W. M. *The Politics of the Private College: An Inquiry into the Processes of Collegiate Government*. New Haven, CT.: Edward W. Hagen Foundation, 1968.

Wood, M. *The Board of Trustees of the Private Liberal Arts College*. Unpublished doctoral dissertation, Harvard University, Cambridge, Mass., 1982.

Woodruff, B. E. "Trustees Must Know the Law." *AGB Reports*, Vol. 18, No. 6, November/December 1976.

Zwingle, J. L. *The Lay Governing Board — Perspectives on Trusteeship*. Washington: Association of Governing Boards, 1970.

Zwingle, J. L. *Effective Trusteeship: Guidelines for Board Members*. Washington: Association of Governing Boards, 1979.

Zwingle, J. L. "Assessing Institutional Performance." In R. T. Ingram (Ed.), *Handbook of College and University Trusteeship*. San Francisco: Jossey-Bass, 1980.

Zwingle, J. L. "Conflict in the Board Room." *AGB Reports*, Vol. 23, No. 4, July/August 1981.

Zwingle, J. L. and Mayville, W. V. *College Trustees: A Question of Legitimacy*. ERIC/ Higher Education Research Report No. 10. Washington: American Association for Higher Education, 1974.

About the Author

John W. Nason has long been recognized as a preeminent authority on problems of academic and foundation governance. He has served as president of Swarthmore College and Carleton College; as trustee of Vassar College, Phillips Exeter Academy, and Carleton College; as a member of the governing boards of the Danforth Foundation and Edward W. Hazen Foundation. He is now a governor of the Bruce L. Crary Foundation.

During his close association with AGB he has written, in addition to this volume, the following books: *The Future of Trusteeship: The Role and Responsibilities of College and University Boards; Presidential Search: A Guide to the Process of Selecting and Appointing College and University Presidents;* and *Presidential Assessment: A Challenge to College and University Leadership.*

A Rhodes Scholar, Dr. Nason attended Oxford, Harvard, Yale Divinity School; received his bachelor's degree from Carleton College in 1926. He and his wife Elizabeth live in Keene, N.Y., in the heart of the Adirondacks.

**Other AGB publications
by John Nason**

Presidential Search
A comprehensive nine-step guide to the selection process, from establishing the search
machinery to making the final choice.

Presidential Assessment
A sequel to Presidential Search, this volume
assists governing boards and presidents in
appraising the relative merits of different
methods of assessment and in developing
guidelines for sound practice.

Trustee Responsibilities
A valuable shorthand guide to the 12 basic
responsibilities of a member of a governing
board. One of AGB's popular "pocket pubs."

About AGB

The Association of Governing Boards of Universities and Colleges (AGB) is a nonprofit educational organization of governing, coordinating, and advisory boards of postsecondary education. AGB exists to help its members fulfill their roles and meet their responsibilities. AGB, among its many functions, emphasizes the elements of good working relationships between administrators and trustees, provides the background information needed by boards to deal with the many critical issues before them, and helps boards function with an awareness of the increasing interdependence of all types of colleges and universities. Founded in 1921. AGB established offices in Washington, D.C., in 1964.

For more information about AGB, including a publications brochure, write to AGB, One Dupont Circle, Suite 400, Washington, D.C. 20036.

Copies of this publication can be ordered by sending a check or money order to AGB. Prices to AGB members: $9.95 ea./$8.95 ea. for orders of 10 or more; nonmembers: $15.00 ea./ $13.50 ea. for orders of 10 or more. Include $1.00 with total order for postage, handling.